*

IRISH PUB
COOKING

LARRY DOYLE

BRISTOL PUBLISHING ENTERPRISES
Hayward , California

A **nitty gritty**® cookbook

Printed in the United States of America.

ISBN 1-55867-309-1

Cover design: Frank J. Paredes
Cover photography: John Benson
Food stylist: Randy Mon
Illustrations: Caryn Leschen

CONTENTS

For Paula and Ryan

THE EVOLUTION OF PUBS AND PUB FOOD

Irish pubs the world over have been going through a serious evolution over the past two decades. The emphasis has shifted away from drink and toward all of the other aspects that make up the pub experience. Perhaps the drinking and driving laws have had an effect, or maybe it's the smoking ban, but one thing is certain: when it comes to spending an evening at the pub, the food has taken center stage. Irish pub goers are demanding reasonably priced, wholesome, freshly and simply prepared comfort food to accompany their favorite beverage. So much so that nowadays the Irish pub has become the equivalent of the French bistro. An unfussy, unpretentious place where people from all economic and cultural backgrounds can enjoy healthy portions of hearty, unintimidating fare in a convivial atmosphere, at a reasonable price, surrounded by the buzz of conversation and, perhaps, the sound of traditional Irish music.

The collection of recipes in this book, some familiar and some new, will inspire you to recreate the Irish pub food experience in your own home. It will also give you an insight into the true nature of Irish cooking, from the straightforward preparations to the essence of Irish flavors. The readily available ingredients and easy-to-follow instructions will allow you quickly and painlessly to prepare wholesome Irish "soul" food with relative ease in your own kitchen.

STOCKS

Good stock is the cornerstone of many recipes. All of these stocks can be made in advance and frozen in small batches for future use.

CHICKEN STOCK

This is the most commonly used stock in this book, and is useful for all kinds of soups and stews.

2 medium carrots, washed and cut into 3-inch-thick slices
2 medium yellow onions, quartered
4 sticks of celery, cut into 3-inch lengths
2 lb. chicken bones (wings tips are best, but backs will do), rinsed in cold, running water and drained
8 cups cold water

Place all ingredients in a large pot over high heat and bring to a boil. Skim and discard foam that rises to the surface, lower heat and simmer very gently for 1 hour, skimming regularly.

Strain stock into a clean container and discard bones and vegetables. Cool completely, cover and refrigerate or freeze until needed.

BEEF STOCK

This rich, tasty stock makes an excellent base for many of the curries and soups in this book. It can be made in advance and frozen for future use.

2 lb. beef bones, rinsed and drained
1/4 cup olive oil
2 medium carrots, peeled, chopped
2 medium yellow onions, peeled and
   quartered

4 sticks celery, chopped
1 cup red wine
1/2 cup tomato paste
8 cups cold water

Heat olive oil in a thick-bottomed pan over high heat. Carefully add bones and brown on all sides. Using tongs, transfer bones to a large stock pot. Add vegetables to pan and brown on all sides. Transfer vegetables to stock pot. Carefully pour hot oil out of pan and discard.

While pan is still hot, pour in red wine and stir to gather food particles left behind in pan. Remove from heat and pour wine into stock pot. Add tomato paste and water to stock pot and bring to a boil over high heat. Skim and discard foam that rises to the surface. Lower heat and simmer very gently for 4 hours, skimming regularly. Strain stock into a clean container and discard bones and vegetables. Cool completely, cover and refrigerate or freeze until needed.

FISH STOCK

This simple stock is suitable for all kinds of soups, pies, and seafood dishes. It can be made in advance and frozen for future use.

2 lb. fish bones and heads, rinsed and drained
1 large leek, washed, quartered lengthways and washed again
2 medium yellow onions, quartered
4 sticks celery, chopped
3 bay leaves
1 tbs. black peppercorns
8 cups cold water

Place all ingredients in a large pot over high heat and bring to a boil. Skim and discard foam that rises to the surface. Lower heat and simmer very gently for 20 minutes, skimming regularly. Turn off heat and allow to cool before draining.

Strain stock into a clean container and discard bones and vegetables. Cool completely, cover and refrigerate or freeze until needed.

SHELLFISH STOCK

Use this stock for many of the seafood stews and curries in this book, or for any seafood recipe where stock is required.

1 lb. fish bones and heads, rinsed and drained

½ lb. fresh mussels

½ lb. shrimp shells, heads and tails if available

1 large leek, washed, quartered lengthways and washed again

2 medium yellow onions, peeled and quartered

4 sticks celery, chopped

3 bay leaves

1 tbs. black peppercorns

8 cups cold water

Place all ingredients in a large pot over high heat and bring to a boil. Skim and discard foam that rises to the surface, lower heat and simmer very gently for 20 minutes, skimming regularly. Turn off heat and allow to cool before draining.

Strain stock into a clean container and discard bones and vegetables. Cool completely, cover and refrigerate or freeze until needed.

MUSHROOM STOCK

This is a good alternative to vegetable stock if you prefer meatless dishes, and better than canned mushroom soup in any dish you care to name.

1 lb. medium brown mushrooms, cleaned
2 medium carrots, peeled and cut into 3-inch thick slices
2 medium yellow onions, quartered
4 sticks celery, cut into 3-inch lengths
4 cloves garlic, smashed
stems from 1 bunch of basil
8 cups cold water

Place all ingredients in a large pot over high heat and bring to a boil. Skim and discard foam that rises to the surface, lower heat and simmer very gently for 20 minutes, skimming regularly. Turn off heat and allow to cool before draining.

Strain stock into a clean container and discard vegetables. Cool completely, cover and refrigerate or freeze until needed.

VEGETABLE STOCK

This stock is quick and easy to prepare. It can be used as a substitute for other stocks in any recipe, or to make a vegetable soup completely vegetarian.

2 medium carrots, peeled, cut into 3-inch thick slices
2 medium yellow onions, quartered
4 sticks celery, cut into 3-inch lengths
1 large leek, washed, quartered lengthways and washed again
4 cloves garlic, smashed
4 sprigs fresh thyme
1 tbs. black peppercorns
8 cups cold water

Place all ingredients in a large pot over high heat and bring to a boil. Skim and discard foam that rises to the surface, lower heat and simmer very gently for 20 minutes, skimming regularly. Turn off heat and cool before draining.

Strain the stock into a clean container and discard vegetables. Cool completely, cover and refrigerate or freeze until needed.

APPETIZERS

Many people come to the pub just for drinks and appetizers. The important thing is to make these dishes small but full of flavor so a wide range can be enjoyed without filling up.

10 Boxty with Smoked Salmon and Dill Cream
12 Crab-Stuffed Mushrooms with Aioli Garlic Mayonnaise
14 Buttermilk Fried Crispy Onion Strings
15 Blue Cheese Toasts
16 Mussels Steamed in Ale
18 Chicken Skewers with Cucumber Sauce
20 Baby Back Ribs in Guinness BBQ Sauce
22 Killer Wings with Gorgonzola Dip
24 Beer-Battered Prawns with Cocktail Sauce
26 Fried Calamari with Chili-Lime Sauce
28 Baked Oysters Samuel Beckett
30 Portobello Mushroom Crostini

BOXTY WITH SMOKED SALMON
AND DILL CREAM

Boxty is a pan-fried potato pancake that originated in County Leitrim. Here it is given a stylish and elegant update.

1 large russet potato, peeled, coarsely grated and drained well
2 cups cold *Mashed Potatoes*, page 61
1 egg, lightly beaten
1 tbs. baking powder
2 cups all-purpose flour
3 tbs. olive oil
salt and ground black pepper to taste
1/2 lb. thinly sliced smoked salmon

Heat one tablespoon of the olive oil in a frying pan until very hot and add in grated potato. Cook, stirring constantly, over high heat, until potato is golden brown. Remove from heat and drain on paper towels. Set aside to cool.

In a large bowl, combine *Mashed Potatoes*, fried grated potato, egg, baking powder, ½ of the flour and salt and pepper. Mix until it forms a ball the consistency of pie dough. Divide mixture into 4 equal parts and roll each one out on remaining flour to ¼-inch thickness.

Heat remaining olive oil in a non-stick pan until hot, lower heat to medium and fry pancakes, one by one, until golden brown. Drain on paper towels, spread each pancake with *Dill Cream*, top with smoked salmon, cut into quarters and serve immediately.

DILL CREAM
½ cup sour cream
2 shallots, peeled and finely chopped
¼ cup finely chopped dill
juice and grated zest of 1 lemon
salt and ground black pepper to taste

In a mixing bowl, combine all ingredients. Mix well and refrigerate until needed.

CRAB-STUFFED MUSHROOMS WITH AIOLI GARLIC MAYONNAISE

Two of Ireland's more prolific foods: crabs and mushrooms are combined here to create a tasty, irresistible snack.

½ lb. fresh lump crabmeat
24 large white mushrooms, cleaned and stems removed
1 medium yellow onion, finely chopped
1 stick celery, finely chopped
1 small red bell pepper, seeded and finely chopped
1 clove garlic, finely chopped
1 cup dry white breadcrumbs
¼ cup mayonnaise
1 tbs. Dijon mustard
1 tbs. olive oil
salt and ground black pepper to taste
Aioli Garlic Mayonnaise, page 122

Heat oven to 375°. Heat olive oil in a skillet until hot and add in onion, celery, bell pepper and garlic. Cook over gentle heat, until vegetables are soft and translucent. Remove from pan and cool completely.

In a bowl, combine cooked vegetables, crabmeat, breadcrumbs, mayonnaise and mustard. Taste and season with salt and pepper.

Fill each mushroom cap to heaping with crab mixture and place on an oiled baking sheet. Bake for 20 to 25 minutes, until mushrooms are soft and stuffing is golden brown on top. Serve hot with a small dollop of *Aioli Garlic Mayonnaise* on top of each one.

BUTTERMILK FRIED CRISPY ONION STRINGS

This is delicious as a shared snack or as a side dish with steaks. You will need a deep-fat fryer to prepare this recipe.

4 medium red onions, very thinly sliced
   into rings
2 cups buttermilk
2 cups all purpose flour
2 cups cornstarch

1 tsp. ground cumin
1 tsp. salt
1 tsp. fine-ground white pepper
1 tbs. course chopped parsley

Heat fryer to 375°. Place onion rings in a deep bowl and completely cover with buttermilk. Marinate for 10 minutes. In another bowl, combine flour, cornstarch, cumin, salt and pepper until well mixed.

Drain onions into a colander, discarding buttermilk. Leaving onions in colander, dust them with flour mixture and toss by hand to coat thoroughly. Over the sink, give the colander a good shake to remove excess flour.

Fry onions in batches in the fryer until golden brown. Remove and drain on paper towels. Season with a little more salt and serve on a platter sprinkled with coarsely chopped parsley.

BLUE CHEESE TOASTS

This is a quick and tasty snack that also doubles as delicious accompaniment to a mixed green salad.

1 sweet baguette, about 18-inch in length
1 cup olive oil
1 clove garlic, peeled
1/2 lb. Maytag blue cheese or Gorgonzola, at room temperature
1/4 lb. butter, at room temperature
black pepper to taste

Heat oven to 375°. With a serrated knife, carefully cut baguette into 20 very even 1/2-inch slices. Lay slices in a single layer on a baking sheet and brush both sides with olive oil. Bake for about 10 minutes, until they are slightly crispy but not browned. Remove from oven and allow to cool. When toasts are cool, gently rub each one with the whole garlic clove to give a garlic flavor.

While toasts are cooking, combine blue cheese and butter until smooth and season with black pepper. Spread cheese mixture neatly onto toasts, arrange attractively on a serving platter and serve immediately.

MUSSELS STEAMED IN ALE

Mussels are highly perishable: use only the freshest you can find. Discard any that are open before you start and closed when you are finished! This is one of those dishes that gets people sitting around a table together and digging in. Quintessential pub food.

2 lb. fresh mussels
2 medium yellow onions, peeled and sliced
2 cloves garlic, peeled and finely chopped
1 stick celery, washed and thinly sliced on the diagonal
1 medium red bell pepper, washed, seeded and thinly sliced
2 tbs. olive oil
3 Roma tomatoes, halved, seeded and cut into small, even dice
1 small pinch chili flakes
2 cups ale
2 cups *Shellfish Stock,* page 6, *Fish Stock,* page 5, or *Chicken Stock,* page 3
¼ cup butter
2 tbs. chopped fresh basil
salt and ground black pepper to taste
1 large lemon, cut into wedges for garnish

Heat olive oil in a large, thick-bottomed pan. Cook onions, garlic, celery and bell pepper in oil over medium heat, stirring constantly, until soft. Add in tomatoes, chili flakes and ale and cook until ale has almost completely evaporated. Add in stock and bring to a simmer. Add mussels and increase heat to high. Cook vigorously until all mussels are opened.

Using a slotted spoon, remove mussels and transfer to a large serving platter. Turn off heat and stir in butter. Add basil and season to taste with salt and pepper. Pour sauce over mussels, arrange lemon wedges around platter and serve immediately.

CHICKEN SKEWERS WITH CUCUMBER SAUCE

Servings: 4

Many Indian influences are to be found in Irish pub food. This one uses a Tandoori spice mixture to create a perfectly lively accompaniment to your favorite beer. The cucumber sauce serves to cool the mouth down and balance the flavors. Bamboo skewers work well for this recipe.

4 chicken breasts, about 6 oz. each, cut into 5
   strips each
¼ cup turmeric
2 tbs. cayenne pepper
¼ cup ground coriander
¼ cup paprika
¼ cup ground cumin
1 tsp. salt
1 tbs. olive oil

Heat oven to 425°. Combine all spices in a small bowl. Carefully work chicken strips onto the bamboo skewers. Lay them out on an oiled baking tray and sprinkle liberally with spice mixture. Turn over and repeat on the other side. Bake for about 8 minutes, until cooked. Serve immediately with *Cucumber Sauce* for dipping.

CUCUMBER SAUCE

1 medium English cucumber, half peeled, split lengthways and seeded
1 clove garlic, coarsely chopped
1 egg yolk
juice of 1 lemon
juice of 1 lime
1 bunch cilantro
¼ cup seasoned rice wine vinegar
½ tsp. Colman's English mustard powder
½ cup olive oil
½ cup plain yogurt
salt and ground black pepper to taste

In a food processor, on fast speed, combine cucumber, garlic, egg yolk, lemon juice, lime juice, cilantro, rice vinegar and mustard powder. When mixture is smooth and green, gradually drizzle in olive oil until incorporated. Add yogurt and process for one more minute until completely combined. Season with salt and pepper. Refrigerate until needed.

BABY BACK RIBS IN GUINNESS BBQ SAUCE

This dish definitely has an Asian feel, but the flavor of the Guinness that comes through in the sauce adds a distinctively Irish element.

2 lb. pork baby-back ribs, split twice lengthwise along the rack (your butcher will do this for you)
4 cups *Chicken Stock*, page 3
4 bay leaves
2 tbs. coriander seeds
2 tbs. yellow mustard seeds

1 pinch chili flakes
¼ cup soy sauce
2 tbs. salt
¼ cup brown sugar, packed
¼ cup olive oil
cilantro sprigs for garnish

Heat oven to 375°. Place ribs in a pan large enough to allow them to be covered with liquid. Combine all other ingredients except olive oil and pour over ribs. Cover with foil or lid and cook for one hour until meat is tender and comes easily off the bone. Remove ribs from liquid, place on a tray and allow to cool completely. Reserve 1 cup of the cooking liquid and discard the rest. When ribs are completely cold, separate them by cutting down between the bones until you have individual, two-bite-sized ribs.

Heat olive oil in a large skillet over high heat. Carefully toss in ribs and cook, tossing and stirring for 2 or 3 minutes, then add in reserved cooking liquid. Continue cooking over high heat until liquid has evaporated. Add in 1 cup of *Guinness Barbecue Sauce*. Toss a few times to coat ribs, remove from heat and serve immediately on a large platter, garnished with cilantro sprigs.

GUINNESS BBQ SAUCE
14 oz. Guinness stout
$1/4$ cup brown sugar, packed
1 large tomato, seeded and finely chopped
$3/4$ cup hoisin sauce (available at most supermarkets)

In a small, thick-bottomed pot, bring Guinness to a boil over high heat. Add in brown sugar and tomato and continue to boil until sauce has reduced by $3/4$. Add hoisin sauce, stirring well, and allow mixture to boil again. Remove from heat, transfer to a blender and puree until smooth. Cool and refrigerate until needed.

KILLER WINGS WITH GORGONZOLA DIP

Servings: 4

One of the most popular dishes to enjoy over drinks, these chicken wings are irresistible. A deep-fat fryer works best for this recipe.

2 lb. chicken wings (select the largest, meatiest ones you can find and remove tips)
1/4 cup olive oil
2 tbs. dried thyme
2 cloves garlic, finely chopped
juice of 1 lemon
1 cup Louisiana hot sauce
1/4 cup butter
juice of 1 lime
1 stalk celery, cut into sticks
1/4 cup chopped scallions for garnish
Gorgonzola Dip, page 23

Heat oven to 375°. In a large bowl, toss wings, oil, thyme, garlic and lemon juice together. Spread on a single layer on a cooking sheet. Bake for about 15 minutes, until cooked but not browned. Remove from oven and transfer to a cooling rack. At this point wings can be cooled completely and refrigerated until needed.

Heat the deep-fat fryer to 375°. Place wings in basket and gently lower into oil. Fry for 5 minutes, until golden brown. Remove from fryer and drain well. Transfer to a large bowl. Immediately add hot sauce and butter and toss until butter has completely melted. Add in lime juice and toss again. Pile wings up on a serving platter. Sprinkle with chopped scallions and serve immediately with celery sticks and *Gorgonzola Dip*.

GORGONZOLA DIP

1 cup mayonnaise
1 bunch basil
1/4 cup sherry vinegar
1/2 cup crumbled Gorgonzola cheese
2 tbs. extra virgin olive oil
salt and ground black pepper to taste

In a blender, combine mayonnaise, basil, vinegar and half of the cheese until smooth. Transfer to a bowl and, using a whisk, stir in remaining cheese and olive oil. Season with salt and pepper. Refrigerate until needed.

BEER-BATTERED PRAWNS
WITH COCKTAIL SAUCE

Servings: 4

For this recipe you will need a deep-fat fryer in order to achieve the desired crispiness of the batter. Use a high quality peanut or canola oil.

1½ lb. prawns, peeled, deveined and tails left on
2 cups all-purpose flour, divided
1½ cups lager beer
2 tbs. parsley, chopped
1 large lemon, cut into wedges
salt and ground white pepper to taste

Heat fryer to 375°. In a large bowl, using a whisk, combine ½ of the flour with beer and most of the parsley. Season to taste. Set aside.

Season prawns with salt and pepper and toss in remaining 1 cup of flour. Shake off excess flour and drop prawns into the batter. Discard flour. Lower the fry basket into oil and carefully drop prawns in one by one. Keep prawns separate for the first minute, until batter has begun to crisp up. This will prevent prawns from sticking together. (Depending on the size of your fryer it may be necessary to cook prawns in batches.) Cook for 3 to 5 minutes, until batter is golden brown. Remove from oil and drain well on paper towels. Place on a serving platter, sprinkle with remaining parsley and garnish with lemon wedges. Serve immediately with *Cocktail Sauce* on the side.

COCKTAIL SAUCE
1 cup ketchup
1/4 cup prepared horseradish
juice of 1 lemon
1 dash Worcestershire sauce
Tabasco Sauce to taste

Combine all ingredients, mix well together and refrigerate until needed.

FRIED CALAMARI WITH CHILI-LIME SAUCE

Once again, you will need a deep-fat fryer to achieve the desired result with this recipe. Calamari is tricky. If overcooked, it will be tough; if undercooked, it will be soggy. It must also be eaten immediately as the crispiness deteriorates as it cools. Great for those times when your guests are milling around the kitchen!

2 lb. calamari tubes and tentacles, cleaned and tubes cut into rings.
1 cup all-purpose flour
1 cup cornstarch
2 tsp. chili powder
1 tsp. ground white pepper
$\frac{1}{2}$ tsp. salt
$\frac{1}{4}$ cup chopped parsley
1 lemon, cut into wedges
Chili-Lime Sauce, page 118

Heat fryer to 375°. In a large mixing bowl, combine flour, cornstarch, chili powder, pepper and salt. Mix well. Toss calamari in flour mixture and transfer to a large colander or strainer. Shake vigorously to remove excess flour.

Immediately fry in hot oil for 2 to 3 minutes, until crispy and golden. Remove from oil and drain on paper towels. Place on a serving dish, sprinkle with parsley and garnish with lemon wedges. Serve immediately with *Chili-Lime Sauce,* page 118, on the side.

BAKED OYSTERS SAMUEL BECKETT

Servings: 4

This dish is a great option for those who prefer their oysters cooked. They can be prepared a day ahead, and baked when needed.

24 medium oysters, washed and shucked, juice and bottom shells reserved
4 cups rock salt
2 tbs. olive oil
4 strips bacon, finely chopped
1 small fennel bulb, trimmed, cored and finely chopped
1 small white onion, finely chopped
1/4 cup Pernod or 1/4 cup dry vermouth and 6 star anise
1 cup heavy cream
1 cup cooked, chopped spinach or 1 pkg. (10 oz.) frozen
1/2 cup parmesan cheese, grated
1 cup white breadcrumbs
salt and ground black pepper

Heat oven to 400°. Spread rock salt on a baking sheet. Heat oil in a thick-bottomed saucepan and add bacon. Cook, stirring, until bacon is crispy. Using a slotted spoon, remove bacon and drain on a paper towel. Set aside. Add fennel and onion to the pan, lower heat and cook, stirring, until soft. Add oyster juice, Pernod and anise and simmer until reduced by $1/2$. Add cream. Bring to a gentle boil, lower heat and simmer until reduced by $3/4$. Add spinach and parmesan cheese, stir well, taste and season with salt and pepper. Remove from heat and allow to cool completely.

Arrange reserved oyster shells on rock salt and place an oyster on each one. Carefully spoon a little of the cream mixture over each oyster and sprinkle with bacon and bread-crumbs. Bake until golden brown and bubbling. Remove from oven, transfer oysters to a platter and serve immediately.

PORTOBELLO MUSHROOM CROSTINI

Servings: 4

This mouth-watering appetizer is so savory and delicious that you'll enjoy making it and serving it time and again.

1 medium sweet baguette
4 portobello mushrooms, peeled, trimmed and very thinly sliced
2 cloves garlic, finely chopped
$^1\!/_2$ cup olive oil
2 tsp. chopped fresh thyme
1 cup red wine
1 cup *Chicken Stock,* page 3
$^1\!/_4$ cup butter
salt and ground black pepper to taste

Heat oven to 375°. With a serrated knife, slice baguette into 1/4-inch-thick slices. Place slices in a large bowl, drizzle with 1/2 of the oil, toss to evenly coat and lay out in a single layer on a baking sheet. Bake for 8 to 10 minutes, until toasted and very lightly golden. Remove from oven and allow to cool.

While crostini are baking, heat remainder of oil in a skillet and add garlic. Add mushrooms and cook, tossing or stirring frequently, until moisture is released. Add thyme, season with salt and pepper and add red wine. Simmer until wine has evaporated, add *Chicken Stock* and simmer until stock is almost evaporated. Remove from heat, stir in butter, taste and season again. Spoon a heaping amount of mushrooms onto crostini and serve immediately.

SOUPS

Soups feature very prominently in Irish cooking. The most important thing is to start with good stock and high-quality ingredients in season. Of course, remember to serve with great bread and lots of butter!

CREAM OF CAULIFLOWER SOUP WITH CRAB

Servings: 4

The smooth texture of the soup provides a wonderful backdrop to the freshness of the crabmeat.

¼ cup plus 2 tbs. olive oil
1 large head cauliflower, trimmed and cut
   into small florets
2 large white onions, sliced
1 clove garlic, sliced
2 tsp. chopped fresh thyme

2 large potatoes, peeled and sliced
4 cups *Chicken Stock,* page 3
½ cup heavy cream
½ lb. fresh lump crabmeat
2 tsp. chopped chives
salt and ground white pepper to taste

Heat ¼ cup oil in a large, thick-bottomed pot. Add onions, lower heat and cook gently, stirring constantly, until soft and translucent. Add cauliflower, garlic, thyme, potatoes and *Chicken Stock.* Increase heat and bring to a boil. Skim, reduce heat, cover with a lid and simmer for 10 to 15 minutes, until potatoes and cauliflower are very soft. Remove from heat and allow to cool slightly. Puree in a blender until very smooth. Stir in cream. Taste, season with salt and pepper and keep warm.

In a small bowl, mix together crabmeat, remaining oil and chives. Divide crab mixture between 4 warm soup bowls and ladle soup in on top. Serve immediately.

ROASTED WINTER VEGETABLE SOUP WITH SAGE CREAM

This is a favorite around Thanksgiving when squashes and sweet potatoes abound.

1 small butternut squash, peeled and cut into 2-inch dice
1 medium sweet potato, peeled and cut into 2-inch dice
1 medium parsnip, peeled and cut into 2-inch dice
1 large carrot, peeled and cut into 2-inch dice
2 small turnips, peeled and cut into 2-inch dice
¼ cup olive oil
1 large white onion, diced
2 cloves garlic, finely chopped
1 sprig fresh sage, chopped
2 sprigs fresh parsley, chopped, for garnish
1 cinnamon stick
1 bay leaf
1 pinch chili flakes
4 cups *Chicken Stock,* page 3
salt and ground black pepper to taste

Heat oven to 400°. Heat oil in a large, thick-bottomed pot and add squash, sweet potato, parsnip, carrot, turnips, onion and garlic. Stir, add sage, parsley and a pinch of salt and pepper. Cook, stirring, for about 5 minutes, then spread in an even layer on a roasting tray and place in oven. Roast for about 45 minutes, stirring occasionally, until vegetables are golden brown.

Return vegetables to pot along with cinnamon stick, bay leaf, chili flakes and *Chicken Stock*. Bring to a boil and skim. Lower heat and simmer, stirring occasionally, for about 30 minutes, until vegetables are well cooked. Remove and discard cinnamon stick and bay leaf. Transfer mixture to a blender and puree until smooth. Taste and season with salt and pepper. Serve in warm bowls with a dollop of *Sage Cream* in the center of each bowl. Sprinkle with chopped parsley.

SAGE CREAM

1 cup heavy cream

2 sprigs fresh sage, chopped

salt and ground white pepper to taste

Whip cream with a wire whisk until stiff. Fold in sage, taste and season with salt and pepper. Refrigerate until needed.

BACON AND CABBAGE CHOWDER

This is a slight twist on the classic Irish dish of bacon and cabbage.

1/2 lb. bacon strips or lean Irish boiling bacon, cut into 1/4-inch dice
1/2 cup butter
1 medium white onion, finely chopped
2 celery sticks, finely diced
1 small head white cabbage, outer leaves removed, cored and finely diced
1/2 cup all-purpose flour
4 cups *Chicken Stock,* page 3, heated
2 large russet potatoes, peeled and cut into 1/4-inch dice
1/2 cup heavy cream
1 tbs. chopped fresh thyme
salt and ground white pepper to taste
2 tbs. chopped parsley for garnish

Melt butter in a thick-bottomed pot over gentle heat and add bacon. Cook, stirring, for 1 minute. Add onion, celery and cabbage. Continue to cook, stirring, over gentle heat, until vegetables are soft and translucent.

Add flour and continue to gently cook, stirring constantly, for about another 2 minutes. Slowly add hot stock while continuing to stir. Increase heat slightly and add potatoes. Bring to a boil, stirring to prevent bottom burning, and skim.

Season with salt and pepper, lower heat and simmer gently for about 10 minutes, stirring occasionally, until potatoes are cooked but not too soft. Remove from heat and check seasoning. Serve immediately in warm bowls, garnished with chopped parsley.

CREAM OF POTATO SOUP
WITH ROASTED GARLIC

Always a big seller whenever we offer this as a soup of the day. The flavor of roasted garlic adds a Mediterranean influence that is very satisfying.

$^1/_2$ cup *Roasted Garlic Puree,* page 113

4 large russet potatoes, peeled and thinly sliced

1 medium white onion, peeled and thinly sliced

2 medium leeks, white part only, well washed and thinly sliced

4 cups *Chicken Stock,* page 3

1 cup chopped fresh parsley

$^1/_2$ cup heavy cream

$^1/_4$ cup olive oil

salt and ground white pepper to taste

Heat oil in a thick-bottomed pot and add in onion and leek. Cook gently, stirring, until soft and translucent. Add in stock, potatoes, garlic puree and a pinch of salt and pepper. Bring to a boil and skim. Lower heat and simmer for 25 minutes, until potatoes are very soft. Remove from heat, allow to cool slightly, then puree in a blender until very smooth. Add in cream, taste, season again with salt and pepper, then stir in most of the parsley. Serve immediately in warm bowls. Garnish with remaining chopped parsley.

CURRIED PEA SOUP WITH HAM

Servings: 4

A slight hint of curry transforms this soup into something sublime and exotic. Frozen peas work well for this recipe but fresh peas in season are much better.

1 lb. garden peas
1/4 cup olive oil
2 large white onions, thinly sliced
2 sticks celery, thinly sliced
2 medium carrots, peeled and thinly sliced
2 cloves garlic, chopped
1/4 cup all-purpose flour

2 tbs. tomato paste
1/4 cup curry powder
4 cups *Chicken Stock*, page 3
1/2 lb. cooked ham, cut into 1/4-inch dice
1 bunch tarragon, stemmed and chopped
salt and ground black pepper to taste

Heat oil in a thick-bottomed pan and add onions, celery, carrots and garlic. Cook gently, stirring, until soft. Stir in flour, tomato paste and curry powder and continue to cook, stirring, for about 3 minutes. Add stock and bring to a boil, stirring constantly to prevent sticking. Add in peas and 1/2 of the tarragon. Season with salt and pepper, skim, lower heat and simmer gently for 30 to 45 minutes, stirring occasionally.

Remove from heat, transfer to a blender and puree until smooth. Return to pot, add ham and bring back to a simmer. Add tarragon, taste and season with salt and pepper. Remove from heat and serve in warm bowls.

BEEF AND GUINNESS SOUP WITH BARLEY

Servings: 4

Ten years ago I added this soup to our menu and it is as well received today as it was then. This is a pub classic.

1 lb. lean ground beef
¼ cup olive oil
1 large white onion, diced
2 sticks celery, cut into ¼-inch dice
2 medium carrots, peeled and cut into
   ¼-inch dice
2 cloves garlic, finely chopped
¼ cup tomato paste
1 pinch chili flakes
3 cups *Beef Stock*, page 4
1 cup Guinness
1 cup pearl barley
salt and ground black pepper to taste
chopped parsley for garnish

Heat oil in a thick-bottomed pot and add ground beef. Cook, stirring, over high heat until browned. Remove to a strainer or colander and allow all of the fat to drain off. Discard fat. Add onion, celery, carrots and garlic to pot and cook gently, stirring until softened.

Return beef to pot and add tomato paste, chili flakes, salt, pepper, Guinness and stock. Bring to a boil, stirring constantly. Add barley. Return to a boil, skim, lower heat and simmer gently for 30 to 45 minutes, stirring occasionally, until barley is plump and softened. Remove from heat, taste and season again with salt and pepper. Serve in warm bowls, garnished with chopped parsley.

SPICY CHICKEN AND VEGETABLE SOUP WITH RICE

Servings: 4

Jose Mukul, my sous chef at Johnny Foley's, developed this soup which has become a firm favorite with our regular customers.

1 lb. cooked chicken
¼ cup olive oil
1 large white onion, peeled
2 medium carrots, peeled
2 sticks celery
3 Roma tomatoes, seeded
1 large russet potato, peeled
2 cloves garlic, chopped
1 jalapeño chile, seeded and finely
   chopped
1 pinch chili flakes
¼ cup chili powder
2 tbs. tomato paste
1 cup white rice
4 cups *Chicken Stock,* page 3

1 bunch cilantro, picked and chopped
salt and ground black pepper to taste

Cut chicken, onion, carrots, celery, tomatoes and potato into ½-inch dice. Heat oil in a thick-bottomed pot and add onion, carrots, celery, tomatoes, garlic and jalapeño. Cook, stirring, for about 4 minutes.

Add chili flakes, chili powder, tomato paste, *Chicken Stock* and ½ of the cilantro. Bring to a boil and add chicken, rice and potatoes. Bring back to a boil, skim and season with salt and pepper. Lower heat and simmer gently for 30 minutes, stirring occasionally.

When potatoes and rice are cooked, remove from heat. Taste, season again with salt and pepper, stir in remaining cilantro and serve in warm bowls.

CARROT AND GINGER SOUP WITH CILANTRO

On a recent trip to Ireland, this was the soup of the day at almost every eatery I visited. Maybe because the three principal ingredients are the colors of the Irish flag!

4 medium carrots, peeled and rough chopped
$1/4$ cup olive oil
2 medium white onions, chopped
2 sticks celery, chopped
2 cloves garlic, peeled and chopped
$1/4$ lb. fresh ginger, chopped

1 bunch cilantro, stemmed and chopped, stems and a few sprigs reserved
4 cups *Chicken Stock,* page 3
1 pinch chili flakes
salt and ground black pepper to taste
$1/4$ cup heavy cream

Heat oil in a thick-bottomed pot and add carrots, onions, celery, garlic, ginger and cilantro stems. Cook gently, stirring, until vegetables are soft. Add in $1/2$ of the cilantro, chili flakes and *Chicken Stock* and bring to a boil. Season with salt and pepper, skim, lower heat and simmer gently for 30 minutes. Remove from heat, transfer to a blender and puree until smooth. Return to pot, stir in remaining cilantro and cream, taste and season with salt and pepper. Serve in warm bowls garnished with cilantro sprigs.

SALADS

One doesn't immediately associate salads with Irish food or pub food, but nowadays, people are eating healthier foods, even when they are relaxing at the pub.

SPINACH SALAD WITH CORNMEAL FRIED EGG

Servings: 4

This is a great brunch item or a very interesting first course. The yolk of the egg acts as the unifying ingredient that brings all the flavors together in your mouth.

1 lb. baby spinach, washed and dried
1 small head frisee, washed, spun and cut into sprigs
1 bulb Belgian endive, end cut off and discarded, outer leaves pulled apart, washed and spun
1 medium red onion, halved and very thinly sliced
3/4 cup *Bacon Vinaigrette*, warmed
8 slices bacon, cooked crisp and cooled
4 freshly cooked, hot, *Cornmeal Fried Eggs*
salt and ground black pepper to taste

In a salad bowl, toss together spinach, frisee, endive, onion and *Bacon Vinaigrette*. Taste and season with salt and ground black pepper. Pick out endive leaves and arrange them attractively like a flower on four plates. Mound salad in the center of each plate. Place 2 strips of bacon criss-cross on top of each salad and top with a *Cornmeal Fried Egg*. Serve immediately.

CORNMEAL FRIED EGGS

4 large eggs, poached for 3 minutes, cooled in ice water and peeled

½ cup all-purpose flour, seasoned to taste with salt and ground black pepper

1 beaten egg, combined with ¼ cup buttermilk

1 cup cornmeal

Heat deep fat-fryer to 350°. Dry eggs on paper towels and coat with seasoned flour. Dip in beaten egg mixture and roll in cornmeal until completely coated. Carefully drop eggs into fryer and cook for about 2 minutes, until golden. Remove from fryer, drain on paper towels and keep warm.

GORGONZOLA AND APPLE SALAD
WITH SPICED WALNUTS

Servings: 4

The combination of gorgonzola cheese, apples and walnuts is always a winner. This salad packs a lot of flavor.

½ lb. spring mix greens, washed and dried in a salad spinner
1 red onion, halved and very thinly sliced
2 medium Granny Smith apples, quartered, cored and thinly sliced with skin on

½ cup *Spiced Walnuts*
½ cup crumbled gorgonzola cheese
½ cup Gorgonzola Dressing
salt and ground black pepper to taste

In a salad bowl, toss greens, onion, apples and *Spiced Walnuts* with dressing. Mix well, taste and season with salt and pepper. Divide between 4 salad plates, sprinkle with Gorgonzola crumbles and serve immediately.

SPICED WALNUTS

2 cups shelled walnut halves
¼ cup butter
½ cup brown sugar, packed
½ tsp. chili powder

½ tsp. curry powder
1 pinch cayenne pepper
1 pinch salt

Heat oven to 375°. Bring a small pot of water to a boil and add walnuts. Bring back to a boil, lower heat and simmer gently for 1 minute. Remove from heat, drain off water and toss in butter, swirling around until walnuts are coated. Add sugar, chili powder and curry powder and toss until nuts are evenly coated.

Transfer to a baking sheet and bake for about 20 minutes, until nuts are crunchy but not too brown. Remove from oven and toss in a bowl with salt and cayenne pepper. Cool completely. Store in an airtight container until needed.

GORGONZOLA DRESSING

¼ cup apple cider vinegar
½ cup extra virgin olive oil
1 tsp. Colman's English Mustard powder

2 shallots, peeled and finely chopped
½ cup crumbled Gorgonzola cheese
salt and ground black pepper to taste

Whisk together vinegar, mustard powder and shallots. While continuing to whisk, slowly drizzle in olive oil until incorporated. Stir in cheese, taste and season with salt and pepper. Refrigerate until needed.

ENDIVE SALAD WITH DUCK LIVER TOASTS

Servings: 4

The bitterness of endives provides a nice balance to the sweet richness of duck livers.

½ lb. mixed endives (radicchio, frisee, Belgian endive), washed and dried

1 medium red onion, halved and thinly sliced

½ pint cherry tomatoes

½ cup dried cranberries, soaked for 15 minutes in hot water

¾ cup *Balsamic Vinaigrette,* page 123

½ lb. cooked, *Chopped Duck Livers*

8 long thick slices of baguette, toasted or grilled

salt and ground black pepper to taste

In a salad bowl, toss together endives, onion, tomatoes and cranberries with *Balsamic Vinaigrette.* Taste, season with salt and pepper and arrange attractively on 4 plates. Spread duck livers on toasts and place 2, criss-crossed, on each plate. Serve immediately.

CHOPPED DUCK LIVERS

½ lb. duck livers, washed and dried
2 shallots, peeled and finely chopped
¼ cup olive oil
½ cup sherry
1 tbs. chopped fresh thyme
kosher salt and ground black pepper to taste

Season livers with salt and pepper. Heat oil in a frying pan and toss in livers. Cook, turning frequently, for about 4 minutes, until browned. Add shallots and sherry. Allow sherry to almost completely evaporate. Add thyme and toss everything together.

Remove from heat and transfer livers to a plate to cool. When cool, chop all livers evenly and mix with any juices that have collected on the cooling plate. Taste, season with salt and pepper and serve.

CRAB, MANGO AND AVOCADO SALAD WITH CURRY AIOLI

Exotic, satisfying and great with a beer, this salad brings many elements together. The Curry Aioli is the grand finale!

1 lb. Dungeness crabmeat, picked through and kept chilled
2 each ripe avocadoes and mangoes, halved, peeled, cut into 1/2-inch dice
juice and zest of 1 lemon
juice and zest of 1 lime
1 red onion, finely chopped
1 small head iceberg lettuce, chopped, washed and dried
1/2 cup olive oil
salt and ground black pepper to taste
1/2 cup *Curry Aioli,* page 53

In a large salad bowl, toss together crabmeat, avocadoes, mangoes, lemon juice and zest, lime juice and zest, onion, lettuce and olive oil. Taste and season with salt and pepper. Divide between 4 cold plates, drizzle with *Curry Aioli* and serve immediately.

CURRY AIOLI

1 egg yolk
1 clove garlic, finely chopped
juice of 1 lemon
$\frac{1}{2}$ cup olive oil
$\frac{3}{4}$ tsp. curry powder
salt to taste
1 pinch cayenne pepper

In a food processor workbowl, combine egg yolk, garlic, lemon juice and curry powder. With the motor running, gradually pour in oil in a thin stream until mixture is the consistency of mayonnaise. Season to taste with salt and cayenne pepper.

ROASTED BEET SALAD
WITH ORANGE VINAIGRETTE

Servings: 4

This is a great winter salad. The addition of watercress and feta cheese adds just the right amount of contrast to round out the flavors.

1 lb. *Roasted Baby Beets*, peeled,
   in ¼-inch slices
2 medium oranges, peeled and cut
   into ¼-inch slices
½ lb. baby watercress
½ cup *Orange Vinaigrette*, page 124
½ cup feta cheese, crumbled
kosher salt and ground black pepper to taste

Divide sliced beets and oranges between 4 cold plates and arrange them alternately overlapping in a circle. In a salad bowl, toss together watercress and vinaigrette. Taste and season with salt and pepper. Place a mound of salad in the middle of each plate. Sprinkle feta cheese on each salad and a little kosher salt and ground pepper on top. Serve immediately.

ROASTED BABY BEETS

1½ lb. assorted baby beets, washed well
¼ cup olive oil
kosher salt and ground black pepper to taste
1 tbs. chopped fresh thyme
1 tsp. chopped fresh rosemary

Heat oven to 400°. In a mixing bowl, toss beets, oil, salt, pepper, thyme and rosemary together. Place them in a single layer in a roasting pan. Cook for 45 minutes until beets are easily pierced with a paring knife. Remove from oven and allow to cool. When cool, gently remove skins by simply peeling them back between your fingers. Refrigerate until needed.

SIMPLE GREEN SALAD
WITH SHERRY VINAIGRETTE

Great as an accompaniment to almost any dish, this basic salad still satisfies on many levels.

½ lb. spring mix greens, washed and dried
1 small red onion, very thinly sliced
½ pint cherry tomatoes

½ cup *Sherry Vinaigrette*
salt and fresh ground black pepper to taste

In a large salad bowl, toss together greens, onions, tomatoes and vinaigrette. Taste and season with salt and pepper. Serve immediately.

SHERRY VINAIGRETTE

¼ cup sherry vinegar
½ cup extra virgin olive oil
1 tsp. Colman's English Mustard powder

2 shallots, peeled and finely diced
salt and ground black pepper to taste

In a large bowl, whisk together vinegar, mustard powder, shallots and a little salt and pepper. While continuing to whisk, slowly drizzle in olive oil until incorporated. Taste and season again with salt and pepper. Refrigerate until needed.

CUCUMBER RAITA YOGURT SALAD

Raitas (salads made with yogurt and chopped vegetables) are popular in India. This is a great example of a food that blends Indian and West European, as the Irish love cucumbers, and so are receptive to them in a somewhat more exotic dish. Combine this simple cucumber salad with the Saffron Rice Pilaf for Curries, *page 73, and any curry dish.*

1 English cucumber, peeled, split length-ways, seeded and cut in $1/4$-inch dice
1 cup plain yogurt
1 clove garlic, finely chopped
1 bunch mint, stemmed and chopped
$1/2$ tsp. ground cumin, toasted
salt and ground black pepper to taste

Combine all ingredients in a bowl. Refrigerate until needed.

PIES

These simple, one-dish meals play a major role in the pub dining experience. The combination of "a pie and a pint" warms many a heart on a chilly day.

SHORTCRUST PASTRY FOR SAVORY PIES

This simple pastry is well-suited to all of the pie recipes in this book.

1 cup all-purpose flour, sifted
¼ cup butter, cut into small chunks
1 pinch salt
¼ cup ice water

In a bowl, blend butter, salt and flour by rubbing between your thumb and fingers until mixture has the consistency of breadcrumbs. Add water and work into a ball. Refrigerate for 30 minutes before using.

COTTAGE PIE WITH MASHED POTATOES

This pie is the most popular of the group, especially with kids. Very comforting and homely.

1 lb. lean ground beef
1/2 cup olive oil
1 large white onion, cut into 1/2-inch dice
2 medium carrots, peeled and cut into 1/2-inch dice
2 sticks celery, cut into 1/2-inch dice
2 cloves garlic, finely chopped
1/2 cup all-purpose flour
1/4 cup tomato paste

2 cups *Beef Stock,* page 4, or *Chicken Stock,* page 3
1 pinch chili flakes
1 tbs. chopped fresh thyme
salt and ground black pepper to taste
4 cups *Mashed Potatoes,* page 61 for topping
1/2 cup chopped parsley for garnish

Heat oven to 375°. Heat oil in a thick-bottomed pan and add beef. Cook, stirring, for about 5 minutes, until browned. Remove to a colander and set aside to allow fat to drain.

Meanwhile, add onion, carrots, celery and garlic to pan and cook, stirring, until slightly browned. Stir in flour and tomato paste and continue to cook, stirring, for 2 minutes. Add stock, chili flakes and thyme. Bring mixture to a gentle boil, stirring constantly.

Return beef to pan, stir well and season with salt and pepper. Lower heat and cook for 30 minutes, stirring occasionally. Remove from heat, taste and season with salt and pepper.

Transfer to a 2-quart casserole, so mixture fills half way. Set aside and allow to cool. When filling has cooled, carefully top with *Mashed Potatoes*, spreading evenly to seal the edges. Fluff the top with a fork and bake for about 30 minutes, until *Mashed Potatoes* are golden brown. Remove from oven, sprinkle with chopped parsley and serve.

MASHED POTATOES
2 large russet potatoes, peeled and quartered
¼ cup butter
½ cup heavy cream
salt and ground white pepper to taste

Place potatoes in a pot, cover with cold water, add a pinch of salt and bring to a boil. Lower heat and simmer for about 15 minutes, until soft. Drain well. Return potatoes to pot, add butter and cream to pot with potatoes and mash well. Taste, season with salt and pepper and keep warm until needed.

SHEPHERD'S PIE

Traditionally, ground, cooked leg of lamb was used to make this pie, but nowadays you can just buy ground lamb and cook the recipe from scratch.

1 lb. lean ground lamb
1/2 cup olive oil
1 large white onion, cut into 1/2-inch dice
2 medium carrots, peeled and cut into 1/2-inch dice
2 sticks celery, cut into 1/2-inch dice
2 cloves garlic, finely chopped
1/2 cup all-purpose flour
1/4 cup tomato paste
2 cups *Beef Stock,* page 4, or *Chicken Stock,* page 3
1 pinch chili flakes
1 tbs. chopped fresh thyme
salt and ground black pepper to taste
4 cups *Mashed Potatoes* for topping, page 61
1/2 cup chopped parsley for garnish

Heat oven to 375°. Heat oil in a thick-bottomed pan and add lamb. Cook, stirring, for about 5 minutes, until browned. Remove to a colander and set aside to allow fat to drain.

Meanwhile, add onion, carrots, celery and garlic to the pan and cook, stirring, until slightly browned. Stir in flour and tomato paste and continue to cook, stirring, for 2 minutes. Add stock, chili flakes and thyme. Bring mixture to a gentle boil, stirring constantly. Add lamb back in, stir well and season with salt and pepper. Lower heat and cook for 30 minutes, stirring occasionally. Remove from heat, taste again and season with salt and pepper.

Transfer to a 2-quart casserole, so that mixture fills half way. Set aside and allow to cool. When filling has cooled, carefully top with *Mashed Potatoes*, spreading evenly to seal edges. Fluff the top with a fork and bake for 30 minutes, until *Mashed Potatoes* are golden brown. Remove from oven, sprinkle with chopped parsley and serve.

STEAK AND MUSHROOM PIE

Use lean, top quality beef to get the best from this dish. Great with a glass of Cabernet Sauvignon.

1 lb. lean beef, cut into 2-inch dice
1/2 cup olive oil
1 lb. medium mushrooms, cleaned and quartered
1 large white onion, cut into 1/2-inch dice
2 medium carrots, peeled and cut
    into 1/2-inch dice
2 sticks celery, cut into 1/2-inch dice
2 cloves garlic, finely chopped
1/2 cup all-purpose flour, plus more for rolling pastry
1/4 cup tomato paste
2 cups *Beef Stock,* page 4, or *Chicken Stock,* page 3
1 pinch chili flakes
1 tbs. chopped fresh thyme
salt and ground black pepper to taste
1 lb. *Shortcrust Pastry for Savory Pies,* page 59, for topping

1 egg, beaten with ¼ cup milk
½ cup chopped parsley for garnish

Heat oven to 375°. Heat oil in a thick-bottomed pan and add beef. Cook, stirring, for about 5 minutes, until browned. Remove from pan and set aside.

Add onion, carrots, celery and garlic to pan and cook, stirring, until slightly browned. Add flour and tomato paste and continue to cook, stirring, for 2 minutes. Add stock, chili flakes and thyme and bring mixture to a gentle boil, stirring constantly.

Return beef to pan, stir well and season with salt and pepper. Lower heat and cook for 30 minutes, stirring occasionally. Add mushrooms and cook for 20 minutes. Remove from heat, taste again and season with salt and pepper.

Transfer to a 2-quart casserole pie dish big enough to hold all the filling. Set aside and allow to cool. When filling has cooled, roll out *Shortcrust Pastry* on a floured board and cover filling completely. Carefully crimp the edge all the way round, then brush top with egg mixture. Bake for 20 minutes, until golden brown. Remove from oven, sprinkle with chopped parsley and serve.

CHICKEN POT PIE

Most people have their own version of this dish. This one has served me well for many years.

1 lb. cooked chicken breasts, in 1-inch dice
½ cup. olive oil
1 large white onion, ½-inch dice
2 medium carrots, peeled in ½-inch dice
2 sticks celery, in ½-inch dice
2 cloves garlic, finely chopped
½ cup all-purpose flour plus more for rolling pastry
2 cups *Chicken Stock,* page 3
1 pinch chili flakes
1 tbs. chopped fresh thyme
1 cup garden peas
salt and ground black pepper to taste
1 egg, beaten with ¼ cup milk
¼ cup Dijon mustard

1 tbs. chopped fresh tarragon
1/2 cup heavy cream
Shortcrust Pastry for Savory Pies, page 59, for topping
1/2 cup chopped parsley for garnish

Heat oven to 375°. Heat oil in a thick-bottomed pan and add onion, carrots, celery and garlic. Cook, stirring, for 3 minutes. Stir in and cook for a further 2 minutes. Gradually add in stock, stirring constantly, until it boils. Lower heat and add chicken, chili flakes, thyme and peas. Stir well, taste and season with salt and pepper.

Simmer gently for 10 minutes. Stir in mustard, tarragon and cream. Taste again, season with salt and pepper and transfer to a pie dish big enough to hold filling. Set aside and allow to cool.

When filling has cooled, roll out *Shortcrust Pastry* on a floured board and cover filling completely. Carefully crimp the edge all the way round. Brush top with egg mixture. Bake for 20 minutes, until golden brown. Remove from oven, sprinkle with chopped parsley and serve.

HUNTER'S PIE

This pie contains venison, a popular item among Irish pub goers and their American counterparts.

1 lb. lean venison, in 2-inch dice
½ cup olive oil
1 large white onion, in ½-inch dice
2 medium carrots, peeled and cut
   into ½-inch dice
2 sticks celery, in ½-inch dice
2 cloves garlic, finely chopped
½ cup all-purpose flour, plus more for rolling pastry
¼ cup tomato paste
2 cups *Beef Stock,* page 4, or *Chicken Stock,* page 3
1 pinch chili flakes
1 tbs. chopped fresh thyme
1 lb. medium mushrooms, cleaned and quartered
salt and ground black pepper to taste

1 lb. *Shortcrust Pastry for Savory Pies,* for topping, page 59
1 egg, beaten with ¼ cup milk
½ cup chopped parsley for garnish

Heat oven to 375°. Heat oil in a thick-bottomed pan and add venison. Cook, stirring, for about 5 minutes, until browned. Remove from pan and set aside.

Add onion, carrots, celery and garlic to pan and cook, stirring, until slightly browned. Stir in flour and tomato paste and continue to cook, stirring, for 2 minutes. Add stock, chili flakes and thyme and bring to a gentle boil, stirring constantly.

Return venison to pan, stir well and season with salt and pepper. Lower heat and cook for 30 minutes, stirring occasionally. Add mushrooms and continue to cook for a further 20 minutes. Remove from heat, taste again and season with salt and pepper.

Transfer to a pie dish big enough to hold all the filling. Set aside and allow to cool. When filling has cooled, roll out *Shortcrust Pastry* on a floured board and cover filling completely. Carefully crimp the edge all the way round, then brush the top with egg mixture. Bake for 20 minutes until golden brown. Remove from oven, sprinkle with chopped parsley and serve.

FISHERMAN'S PIE

A popular dish around Killybegs in County Donegal, this pie is perfect for a blustery day by the seaside.

1 lb. cod, haddock or halibut, in 1-inch dice

$1/2$ lb. prawns, peeled, deveined and in 2-inch pieces

$1/4$ lb. smoked cod, in 1-inch dice

2 large white onions, in $1/2$-inch dice

2 sticks celery, in $1/2$-inch dice

2 cups garden peas

2 cloves garlic, finely chopped

$1/2$ cup olive oil

$1/2$ cup all-purpose flour plus more for rolling pastry.

2 cups *Fish Stock*, page 5

1 pinch chili flakes

1 tbs. chopped fresh chives

$1/2$ cup heavy cream

salt and ground white pepper to taste

1 lb. *Shortcrust Pastry for Savory Pies,* for topping, page 59

1 egg, beaten with $1/4$ cup milk

$1/2$ cup chopped parsley for garnish

Heat oven to 375°. Heat oil in a thick-bottomed pan and add onions, celery and garlic. Cook, stirring, for 3 minutes. Stir in flour and cook for a further 2 minutes. Gradually add stock, stirring constantly until it boils.

Lower heat and add fish, prawns, chili flakes and peas. Stir well, taste and season with salt and pepper. Return to a simmer and simmer gently for 10 minutes. Stir in chives and cream. Taste again, season with salt and pepper and transfer to a pie dish big enough to hold all the filling.

Set aside and cool. When filling has cooled, roll out *Shortcrust Pastry* on a floured board and cover filling completely. Carefully crimp the edge all the way round, then brush top with egg mixture. Bake for 20 minutes, until golden brown. Remove from oven, sprinkle with chopped parsley and serve.

CURRIES

Indian influences came to Irish cooking via the British occupation of India. Irish pub goers love the combination of curry and beer. Pub curries are generally made with Madras Curry Powder and are not overly spicy but balanced with sweetness.

SAFFRON RICE PILAF FOR CURRIES

This simple rice pilaf makes a perfect accompaniment for any curry dish. Serve with Cucumber Raita Yogurt Salad, page 57.

2 tbs. butter
1 medium white onion, in ¼-inch dice
1 stick celery, in ¼-inch dice
1 cup basmati rice, rinsed and drained
1 good pinch saffron threads
1¾ cups *Chicken Stock,* page 3
salt and ground black pepper to taste

Melt butter in a thick-bottomed pot and add onion and celery. Cook, stirring, for 3 minutes, until softened. Add rice, saffron and stock. Bring to a boil and stir well. Lower heat, cover with a tight-fitting lid and simmer very gently for about 10 minutes. When all stock has been absorbed, turn off heat and fluff rice gently with a fork. Taste, season with salt and pepper and serve immediately.

CHICKEN CURRY

The most popular of the curries, this one calls for chicken thighs, which add more depth of flavor. Serve with Saffron Rice Pilaf for Curries, *page 73, and* Cucumber Raita Yogurt Salad, *page 57.*

½ cup olive oil
2 large white onions, in ½-inch slices
2 medium carrots, peeled, in ½-inch dice
2 sticks celery, in ½-inch dice
3 cloves garlic, finely chopped
½ cup curry powder
½ cup all-purpose flour
½ cup tomato paste
4 cups *Chicken Stock,* page 3
½ cup sugar
salt and ground black pepper to taste
½ cup plain yogurt
1 lb. boneless chicken thighs, in 2-inch dice
cilantro sprigs for garnish

Heat oil in a large, thick-bottomed pan and add onions, carrots, celery and garlic. Cook, stirring, for 3 minutes. Stir in curry powder, flour and tomato paste. Continue to cook, stirring, for 3 minutes. Add stock. Bring to a boil, stirring constantly, and lower heat. Stir in sugar, taste, season with salt and pepper and simmer for 30 minutes, stirring occasionally.

Remove from heat and puree in a blender until very smooth. Return sauce to pot and add chicken. Cook gently, stirring occasionally, for 25 minutes, until chicken is done. Remove from heat, stir in yogurt, taste again and season with salt and pepper. Garnish with cilantro sprigs.

BEEF CURRY

Although not something you would find too easily in India, beef curry is certainly a popular item in pubs. Great with an ice cold beer or cider. Serve with Saffron Rice Pilaf for Curries, *page 73, and* Cucumber Raita Yogurt Salad, *page 57.*

1 lb. lean beef chuck, in 2-inch dice
½ cup olive oil
2 large white onions, in ½-inch slices
2 medium carrots, peeled , in ½-inch dice
2 sticks celery, in ½-inch dice
3 cloves garlic, finely chopped
½ cup curry powder
½ cup all-purpose flour
½ cup tomato paste
4 cups *Beef Stock*, page 4
½ cup granulated sugar
½ cup plain yogurt
salt and ground black pepper to taste
cilantro sprigs for garnish

Heat oil in a large, thick-bottomed pan and add beef. Cook, stirring, for 5 minutes, until browned on all sides. Remove meat and set aside.

Add onions, carrots, celery and garlic to pan and cook, stirring, for 3 minutes. Add curry powder, flour and tomato paste. Continue to cook, stirring, for 3 minutes. Add stock. Bring to a boil, stirring constantly. Lower heat, stir in sugar, taste and season with salt and pepper. Simmer for 30 minutes, stirring occasionally.

Remove from heat and puree in a blender until very smooth. Return sauce to pot and add cooked beef. Cook gently, stirring occasionally, for 30 minutes, until meat is tender. Remove from heat, stir in yogurt, taste again and season with salt and pepper. Garnish with cilantro sprigs. Serve immediately.

LAMB CURRY

The flavor and texture of lamb lends itself wonderfully to all sorts of robust cooking styles and flavors. The addition of cilantro, basil and mint to this recipe rounds out the exotic flavors. Serve with Saffron Rice Pilaf for Curries, page 73, and Cucumber Raita Yogurt Salad, page 57.

1 lb. lean, boneless stewing lamb, in 2-inch dice
2 large white onions, in ½-inch slices
2 medium carrots, peeled, in ½-inch dice
2 sticks celery, in ½-inch dice
3 cloves garlic, finely chopped
½ cup olive oil
½ cup curry powder
½ cup all-purpose flour
½ cup tomato paste
4 cups *Beef Stock*, page 4
½ cup granulated sugar
½ cup plain yogurt
1 bunch cilantro, chopped

1 bunch mint, stemmed and chopped
1 bunch basil, stemmed and chopped
salt and ground black pepper to taste

Heat oil in a large, thick-bottomed pan and add lamb. Cook, stirring, for 5 minutes, until browned on all sides. Remove meat and set aside.

Add onions, carrots, celery and garlic and cook, stirring, for 3 minutes. Add curry powder, flour and tomato paste. Continue to cook, stirring, for 3 minutes. Add stock. Bring to a boil, stirring constantly and lower heat. Stir in sugar, taste, season with salt and pepper and simmer for 30 minutes, stirring occasionally.

Remove from heat and puree in blender until very smooth. Return sauce to pot and add lamb. Cook gently, stirring occasionally, for 30 minutes, until meat is tender. Remove from heat, stir in yogurt, cilantro, mint and basil. Taste again and season with salt and pepper. Garnish with cilantro. Serve immediately.

SEAFOOD CURRY

The easy part about this recipe is that once the sauce is made, it is simply a matter of adding in your favorite variety of fresh seafood and it's ready in 10 minutes. Serve with Saffron Rice Pilaf for Curries, *page 73, and* Cucumber Raita Yogurt Salad, *page 57.*

½ cup olive oil
2 large white onions, in ½-inch slices
2 medium leeks, washed well, halved lengthways, in ½-inch slices
2 sticks celery, in ½-inch dice
3 cloves garlic, finely chopped
½ cup curry powder
½ cup all-purpose flour
¼ cup tomato paste
4 cups *Shellfish Stock,* page 6
½ cup granulated sugar
salt and ground black pepper to taste
½ lb. fresh cod or halibut, in 2-inch pieces
¼ lb. prawns, peeled and deveined

¼ lb. mussels, cleaned
½ cup plain yogurt
1 bunch cilantro, chopped

Heat oil in a large, thick-bottomed pan and add onions, leeks, celery and garlic. Cook, stirring, for 3 minutes. Stir in curry powder, flour and tomato paste. Continue to cook, stirring, for 3 minutes.

Add stock. Bring to a boil, stirring constantly. Lower heat and stir in sugar. Taste, season with salt and pepper and simmer for 30 minutes, stirring occasionally. Remove from heat and puree in a blender until very smooth.

Return sauce to pot and add fish and shellfish. Cook gently, stirring occasionally, for 10 minutes, until fish is done and mussels are open. Remove from heat and stir in yogurt and cilantro. Taste again and season with salt and pepper. Garnish with cilantro. Serve immediately.

FISH

Being an island surrounded by bountiful waters has made fish and seafood an integral part of Irish daily life. This influence has, of course, ended up in the pub!

GRILLED TROUT WITH HERB SALSA

Ireland's lakes abound with trout. This recipe is simple, quick and easy to prepare.

4 whole ½ lb. trout, head on, gutted, cleaned and butterflied
½ cup olive oil
1 bunch parsley, chopped
1 bunch basil, chopped
¼ cup capers

2 shallots, peeled and finely chopped
1 clove garlic, peeled and finely chopped
12 salted anchovies, finely minced
2 lemons, 1 zested and juiced, 1 sliced for garnish
salt and ground black pepper to taste

Heat grill to very hot. Lay fish flat on a tray. Brush on both sides with ½ of the oil and season with salt and pepper. Set aside. In a bowl, combine the parsley, basil, capers, shallots, garlic, anchovies, lemon juice, lemon zest and remaining oil. Stir well, taste and season with salt and ground black pepper. Set aside to marinate.

Meanwhile, lay fish out on grill, skin side up. Cook for 2 minutes. Lift up, quarter turn fish and lay skin side up. Cook for 2 minutes, then flip over and cook for a further 2 minutes (6 minutes total). Remove fish from grill and place on a serving platter. Smear with herb salsa and garnish with lemon slices. Serve immediately.

FISH AND CHIPS IN LAGER BATTER

By far the most popular dish on any pub menu, this one is easy to prepare and great with a nice cold beer.

1½ lb. fresh cod or halibut, bones removed, in twelve 2-ounce pieces
2 cups all-purpose flour, divided
2 tbs. chopped parsley
1½ cups lager beer
2 lb. russet potatoes, peeled in ½-inch chips
2 large lemons, in wedges
salt and ground white pepper to taste
canola oil for frying

Heat deep-fat fryer to 325°. Fry potatoes for about 10 minutes, until soft in the center but not browned. Drain well on paper towels and let cool. Increase fryer temperature to 375°.

To make batter, mix together ½ of the flour with lager and ½ of the parsley. Taste and season with salt and pepper. Place remaining flour in a shallow container and season with salt and pepper. Pass pieces of fish through seasoned flour and thoroughly coat with batter before carefully dropping them into fryer.

Fry in two batches for about 5 to 8 minutes, until golden brown. Drain well on paper towels. Keep warm. Return temperature of fryer to 325°. Fry potatoes a second time until golden brown and crisp.

Drain well on paper towels, season with a little salt and divide between four plates. Arrange fish on plates, sprinkle with chopped parsley, garnish with lemon wedges and serve with *Tartar Sauce,* page 115, and *Coleslaw,* page 112, on the side.

SMOKED COD WITH ONION CREAM SAUCE

Servings: 4

Smoked cod is very popular among Irish people and is available in every local grocery store on Fridays. This preparation pairs it with an onion cream sauce that balances and mellows out the smokey flavor of the fish. A decidedly Irish flavor.

2 lb. smoked cod (available by order at upscale food markets)
2 cups whole milk
1/4 cup butter

2 white onions, halved and thinly sliced
1/4 cup all-purpose flour
salt and ground white pepper to taste
chopped parsley for garnish

Heat oven to 400°. Pick the pin bones out of fish with pliers and discard. Lay fish in a single layer in a baking dish and pour on 1/2 of the milk. Bake for 20 minutes, until fish is flaky and firm to the touch. Remove from oven and keep warm.

Meanwhile, melt butter in a thick-bottomed pot and add onions. Cook gently, stirring, for 10 minutes, until soft and translucent. Stir in flour and cook, stirring constantly, for a further 3 minutes. Add remaining milk, stirring vigorously while bringing to a boil. Reduce heat and simmer very gently for 10 minutes, stirring very frequently. Taste and season with salt and pepper. Place fish on four warm plates and cover with sauce. Sprinkle with chopped parsley and serve.

ALMOND-BLACK PEPPER CRUSTED SALMON

Servings: 4

The ubiquitous salmon is a favorite of many and this preparation is so easy and foolproof, you'll be serving it at dinner parties for years! Serve with Saffron Butter Sauce, *page 117.*

¼ cup olive oil
2 lb. salmon fillet, cut crossways into 4
   even portions
kosher salt to taste
¼ cup. butter, melted
½ cup. sliced almonds
¼ cup fresh cracked black pepper

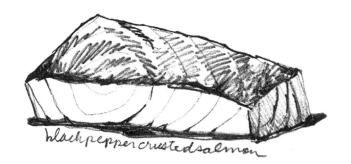

black pepper crusted salmon

Heat oven to 375°. Brush a baking sheet with oil and lay in salmon pieces side by side. Season each piece with a sprinkle of kosher salt. Brush each with plenty of melted butter. Cover each piece of fish with a mound of almonds and press into butter to form a loose crust. Sprinkle with cracked pepper. Bake for 12 minutes, until fish is cooked through and almonds are golden brown. Remove from oven, place on 4 warm plates and serve with *Saffron Butter Sauce,* page 117.

SEAFOOD STEW
WITH ROASTED PEPPER TOASTS

Servings: 4

This hearty coastal dish is a real winner, but the addition of the oysters at the end imparts a surprising flavor of the sea.

½ cup olive oil

1 large white onion, halved and thinly sliced

4 cloves garlic, finely chopped

8 Roma tomatoes, seeded and in ½-inch dice

1 bunch basil, stemmed and chopped

1 pinch chili flakes

1 cup dry vermouth

4 cups *Shellfish Stock,* page 6

salt and ground black pepper to taste

12 oysters, washed well

1½ lb. boneless cod or halibut fillet, in 4 oz. pieces

⅓ lb. mussels, cleaned

⅓ lb. Manila clams

8 crab claws

4 lemons, halved, for garnish

Heat oil in a large pot and add in onion and garlic. Cook gently, stirring, for 4 minutes until soft. Add tomatoes, ½ of the basil, chili flakes and vermouth. Simmer for 5 minutes. Add *Shellfish Stock.* Season lightly with salt and pepper and bring to a boil. Lower heat and simmer gently for 15 minutes.

Add cod or halibut and continue to simmer for 6 minutes. Add mussels, clams and crab claws. Simmer for a further 3 minutes. Add oysters and simmer for another 3 minutes. Stir in remaining basil, taste, season again with salt and pepper and remove from heat.

Arrange fish and shellfish in a large serving bowl and pour on cooking liquid. Garnish with lemon halves and serve immediately with *Roasted Pepper Toasts* on the side for dipping.

ROASTED PEPPER TOASTS

1/4 cup water
1 pinch saffron
1 red bell pepper, roasted, cooled, peeled and seeded
1 cup *Aioli Garlic Mayonnaise,* page 122

salt and ground black pepper to taste
1 baguette, cut on an angle into long, 1/2-inch thick slices
1/4 cup olive oil

Heat oven to 400°. Heat water and pour over saffron. Allow to steep for 5 minutes. In a blender, puree red bell pepper, Aioli and saffron water. Taste and season with salt and pepper. Lay slices of bread in a single layer on a baking sheet and brush on both sides with oil. Bake for 10 minutes, until toasted and lightly golden. Remove from oven and allow to cool. Smear toasts with roasted pepper aioli and serve immediately.

PAN ROASTED MACKEREL WITH BRAISED LEEKS

If you can get really fresh mackerel in season, it has unbelievable flavor and delicacy.

4 medium sized mackerel, 12–14 oz. each, heads removed, gutted and cleaned
½ cup all-purpose flour, seasoned with salt and ground black pepper
1 lemon, thinly sliced
½ cup butter
salt and ground black pepper to taste

Melt butter in a large skillet. Season mackerel with salt and pepper and roll in seasoned flour. When butter is hot, carefully lay each fish side by side and lower heat. Cook fish for 8 minutes on first side. Turn over and cook for 8 minutes. When golden brown and firm to the touch, carefully lift fish out of pan one by one and place on warm plates. Garnish with lemon slices and serve with boiled potatoes and *Braised Leeks,* page 111.

POULTRY AND MEAT

These dishes tend to be robust and rustic, as is the nature of many a pub goer! This is the kind of food that satisfies a hearty appetite.

ROAST CHICKEN WITH CHAMP
AND WHISKEY GRAVY

Use small, 2 lb. chickens and serve ½ of each chicken per portion. Serve this with Whiskey Gravy, *page 116.*

2 small chickens, about 2 lb. each
½ cup olive oil
kosher salt and ground black pepper to taste
6 sprigs rosemary
12 cloves garlic, peeled
2 lemons, halved

Heat oven to 375°. Wash chickens inside and out under cold running water. Dry with paper towels. Place on a roasting tray and rub all over inside and out with oil. Season inside and out with salt and pepper. Place 3 sprigs of rosemary and 6 cloves of garlic inside the cavity of each chicken. Squeeze lemon juice all over inside and outside of chickens, then stuff two lemon halves into each chicken to hold in garlic and rosemary. Roast for 45 minutes. Remove from oven, place chickens on a warm platter and set aside to rest before serving.

CHAMP

2 large russet potatoes, peeled and quartered
¼ cup butter
½ cup heavy cream
1 bunch scallions, chopped
1 bunch parsley, chopped
salt and ground white pepper to taste

Place potatoes in a pot, cover with cold water, add a pinch of salt and bring to a boil. Lower heat and simmer for about 15 minutes, until soft. Drain well. Return to pot, add butter and cream mash well. Add scallions and parsley and stir well. Taste, season with salt and pepper and keep warm until needed.

BRAISED RABBIT WITH PARSNIP PUREE

Servings: 4

This is very much a country dish. People who like this dish love it. I usually offer this with Parsnip Puree, page 109, for a real country meal.

1 rabbit, cleaned, dressed and quartered
salt and ground black pepper to taste
1 tbs. chopped fresh rosemary
$1/2$ cup all-purpose flour
$1/2$ cup olive oil
2 large white onions, in $1/2$-inch dice
4 medium carrots, peeled, in $1/2$-inch dice
4 sticks celery, in $1/2$-inch dice
2 cloves garlic, finely chopped
2 cups *Chicken Stock,* page 3
1 cup white wine
1 pinch chili flakes
chopped parsley for garnish

Heat oven to 350°. Place rack on lower shelf. Cut up the rabbit quarters into 4 pieces each along natural joint lines and place in a bowl. Season with salt and pepper and sprinkle $1/2$ of the rosemary. Add in $1/2$ of the flour and, using both hands, toss rabbit pieces around until evenly coated.

Heat oil in a thick-bottomed, ovenproof pan and carefully add rabbit, piece by piece. Cook, moving pieces around constantly, until browned. Remove to a platter and set aside.

Add onions, carrots, celery and garlic to pan and cook, stirring, for 5 minutes, until slightly browned. Stir in remaining flour and continue to cook, stirring, for 3 minutes. Add in stock, wine and chili flakes and bring to a boil, stirring constantly.

Add rabbit back in, along with any juices that collected on the plate. Return to a boil, skim, taste and season with salt and pepper. Cover, remove from heat and place on lower shelf of oven. Cook for 45 minutes. Remove from oven, taste, season again and stir in remaining rosemary. Serve family-style in a large serving bowl.

TRADITIONAL IRISH LAMB STEW
WITH LITTLE BOILED POTATOES

A very popular dish in Ireland and always a big hit with the tourists, this one is the essence of Irish home cooking. The stew is thickened with potatoes.

2 lb. lean stewing lamb, boneless neck pieces, in 2-inch pieces
3 large white onions, quartered
4 medium carrots, peeled and quartered
2 large russet potatoes, peeled and roughly chopped
4 cups *Chicken Stock,* page 3
2 bay leaves
1 pinch chili flakes
1 tsp. dried thyme
salt and ground white pepper to taste
chopped parsley for garnish

Place meat in a large pot along with onions, carrots, potatoes, stock, bay leaf, chili flakes and thyme. Bring to a boil. Skim well and season with salt and pepper. Lower heat and simmer gently for 45 minutes, skimming and stirring occasionally. When meat is tender, remove piece by piece, along with onions, carrots and bay leaves and set aside. Discard the bay leaves.

Place remaining cooking liquid and potatoes in a blender container and puree until smooth. Return to pot and add meat, onions and carrots back into the liquid. Taste again and season with salt and pepper. Serve in warm bowls with *Little Boiled Potatoes in their Jackets*.

LITTLE BOILED POTATOES IN THEIR JACKETS
12 small Yukon Gold potatoes, washed well
salt and ground white pepper to taste
1/4 cup butter
2 tbs. chopped fresh mint

Place potatoes in a pot and cover with cold water. Add a pinch of salt and bring to a boil. Lower heat and simmer gently for 20 minutes, until potatoes are easily pierced with a knife. Drain well and toss in a bowl with butter, mint, salt and pepper. Serve hot.

PAN-FRIED LAMB'S LIVER
WITH GRILLED ONIONS

Irish mothers serve this to their kids because of the high content of iron and minerals in the liver. Most people really don't appreciate the flavor until they are older. The important thing to do here is not to overcook the meat. Medium-rare to medium is best. Another trick is to soak the liver overnight in milk in the refrigerator. This draws out any strong flavors and enriches the meat.

2 lb. lamb's liver, in 1-inch-thick slices
salt and ground black pepper to taste
1/2 cup all-purpose flour
1/4 cup olive oil

1/2 cup red wine
1 cup *Beef Stock*, page 4
2 tbs. butter
chopped parsley for garnish

Dry liver between paper towels and season with salt and pepper. Dust on both sides with flour. Heat oil in a large skillet and carefully lay in slices of liver. Lower heat to medium and cook liver for 6 minutes, turning once 1/2 way through. Transfer meat to a warm plate and keep warm.

Pour excess juices and fat out of skillet and discard. Return to heat and pour on red wine. Stir well to pick up flavor particles and allow wine to reduce by ³⁄₄. Add stock and reduce by ¹⁄₂ over high heat. Remove from heat, stir in butter, taste and season with salt and pepper. Ladle sauce over liver and serve immediately with *Mashed Potatoes*, page 61, and *Grilled Onions*.

GRILLED ONIONS
2 medium red onions, in ¹⁄₂-inch slices
2 tbs. olive oil
1 tbs. chopped fresh rosemary
salt and ground black pepper to taste

Heat grill to medium heat. Place onions in a large bowl and toss with oil, rosemary and salt and pepper. Let sit for 5 minutes. Place onion slices on grill and cook for 10 minutes, turning frequently. Remove from grill and break into individual rings. Serve immediately.

CORNED BEEF, CABBAGE AND POTATO WRAP

Servings: 4

The elements of this can be prepared a day in advance, making the final dish easier.

2 large heads green cabbage, outer leaves removed, inner leaves finely chopped
¼ cup butter
1 medium white onion, halved and finely chopped
salt and ground white pepper to taste

1 lb. thinly sliced, cooked corned beef
3 cups *Béchamel Sauce,* page 119
2 medium russet potatoes, peeled, in ½-inch dice, cooked and cooled
4 tsp. whole grain Dijon mustard
½ cup chopped parsley

Cook outer leaves of cabbage in boiling salted water for 5 minutes. Rinse under cold water, pat dry and set aside. Melt butter in a thick-bottomed pot; add onion and chopped cabbage. Season with salt and pepper. Cook gently, stirring, for 5 minutes. Remove from heat and cool completely.

In a large bowl, combine meat, 1 cup of the *Béchamel Sauce,* potatoes, cabbage and onion mixture, mustard and ¾ of the parsley. Mix well, taste and season again with salt and pepper if needed. Lay outer leaves of cabbage on a clean surface, dividing them into 4 equal 9-inch squares. Place a mound of meat mixture in center of each square, carefully fold in sides to center and then roll ends up to resemble a burrito. Wrap each roll well with plastic wrap, tying ends into a knot. Bring a pot of salted water to boil and add in 4 cabbage rolls.

Simmer gently for 30 minutes. Meanwhile, heat remaining *Béchamel Sauce* and pass through a fine strainer. Place a pool of sauce in the center of each plate. Lift wraps out of water, carefully remove plastic and, using a spatula, place rolls on plates on top of sauce. Drizzle each plate with *Mustard Vinaigrette,* page 122, sprinkle with chopped parsley and serve immediately.

cabbage rolls...

ROAST TENDERLOIN OF PORK WITH CIDER SAUCE

Pork tenderloin is lean, tender and cooks quickly, making this an easy dish. The cider sauce brings together the flavor of apples and pork. I like to serve this with Rhubarb Relish, page 121.

2 pork tenderloins, 12–16 oz. each, trimmed well
kosher salt and ground black pepper to taste
2 tsp. fresh rosemary, chopped
1/4 cup olive oil
rosemary sprigs for garnish

Heat oven to 425°. Rub pork all over with salt, pepper and rosemary. Heat oil in a large skillet and add in pork. Brown meat on all sides and carefully place skillet in center of oven. Cook for 10 minutes, turning once, to an internal temperature of 145° at the thickest part. Remove skillet from oven and transfer meat to a warm platter. Cover and allow to rest for 10 minutes. Cut meat into 1-inch slices and arrange on platter. Pour on some *Cider Sauce*, garnish with rosemary sprigs and serve immediately with *Rhubarb Relish* on the side.

CIDER SAUCE

1 medium white onion, in ½-inch dice
1 medium carrot, in ½-inch dice
1 stick celery, peeled, in ½-inch dice
2 cloves garlic, chopped
2 shallots, peeled and chopped
1 sprig rosemary
2 cups hard cider
¼ cup. butter
2 cups *Chicken Stock,* page 3
salt and ground black pepper to taste

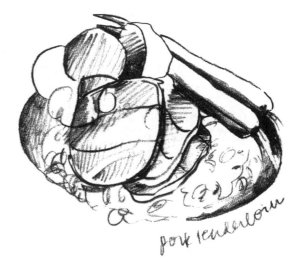

pork tenderloin

Place onion, carrot, celery, garlic, shallots, rosemary and cider in a sauce pan and cider and bring to a boil. Simmer for 15 minutes, until cider has reduced by ½. Add stock and whisk in butter. Bring back to a boil, skim and simmer for 20 minutes, until reduced by ¾. Remove from heat. Taste, season with salt and pepper and pass through a fine strainer. Keep warm.

GLAZED HAM HOCKS WITH ORANGE GLAZE

Serve this with Creamed Cabbage, *page 110, as any combination of brined meat and cabbage is a flavor beloved of the Irish. This delightful dish takes it to the next level while retaining its rustic charm.*

4 small ham hocks, about 1 lb. each
1 medium white onion, in ½-inch dice
1 medium carrot, peeled, in ½-inch dice
1 stick celery, in ½-inch dice
1 tbs. black peppercorns
2 tbs. mustard seeds
6 whole cloves
1 cup sweet white wine
¼ cup *Orange Glaze*
salt and pepper to taste

Heat oven to 375°. Place ham hocks in a pot, cover with cold water and bring to a boil. Remove ham hocks and discard water. Place ham hocks in a braising dish with onion, carrot, celery, peppercorns, mustard seeds, cloves and a pinch of salt and cover again with cold water. Bring to a boil, skim, cover and place in center of the oven. Cook for 1 hour, until meat is tender and about to fall off the bone. Remove from oven, transfer meat to a platter and allow to cool. Strain cooking liquid and reserve. When meat is cool, carefully remove skin and small bone and discard. Place in a baking dish and brush all over with *Orange Glaze*. Place in oven for 10 minutes until glaze is bubbling. Remove from oven and serve.

ORANGE GLAZE

juice and grated zest of 4 oranges
1 star anise pod
1 cinnamon stick

1 pinch chili flakes
1 sprig fresh thyme
1 tsp. sugar

Place all ingredients in a small pot and bring to a boil. Simmer for 10 minutes until reduced by ¾. Strain through a fine strainer and allow to cool.

PEPPERED STEAKS WITH RED WINE SAUCE AND COUNTRY POTATOES

Servings: 4

Whether you prefer, New York, filet mignon, ribeye or T-bone, the important thing is to select good steaks and cook them perfectly. Then all you need is a great potato side dish and a rich, full-bodied red wine.

4 steaks, 2-inch thick, 12–16 oz. each
¼ cup olive oil
kosher salt and ground black pepper
chopped parsley for garnish

Heat grill to medium-high. Brush steaks with oil and season well on both sides with salt and pepper. Grill for 5 minutes each side for medium rare, turning once. Remove from grill and serve immediately with *Country Potatoes,* page 107, and *Red Wine Sauce,* page 120.

COUNTRY POTATOES

16 small Yukon Gold potatoes
1/4 cup olive oil
kosher salt and ground black pepper to taste
chopped parsley for garnish

Cook potatoes in plenty of boiling salted water, until tender but not soft. Drain and cool completely. Slice cold potatoes 1-inch thick. Heat oil in a large skillet and add potatoes in a single layer. Cook quickly, turning once, until crisp and golden. Remove from pan and drain on paper towels. Season with salt and pepper and sprinkle with parsley. Serve at once.

VEGETABLE SIDE DISHES

PARSNIP PUREE

This is perfect with Braised Rabbit, *page 94, but parsnips are a lovely, mild alternative to carrots and this puree is good with almost anything.*

4 large parsnips, peeled and roughly chopped
2 medium russet potatoes, peeled and roughly chopped
1 pinch salt
¼ cup butter
¼ cup heavy cream
salt and ground white pepper to taste

Place parsnips and potatoes in a pot, cover with cold water, add a pinch of salt and bring to a boil. Lower heat and simmer for about 15 minutes, until soft. Drain well. Return to pot and add butter and cream. Mash well until smooth. Taste, season with salt and pepper and keep warm.

CREAMED CABBAGE

I usually serve this with Glazed Ham Hocks with Orange Glaze, *page 104, but it is good as a side for any meat dish.*

1 large head green cabbage, cored, thinly sliced, washed well and drained
1/4 cup butter
2 medium white onions, halved and sliced 1/4-inch thick
1/2 cup sour cream
1 pinch nutmeg
salt and ground white pepper to taste

Cook cabbage for 8 minutes in plenty of boiling, salted water. Drain well and set aside. In a large pan, melt butter and add onion. Cook gently, stirring, for 5 minutes, until soft. Add cabbage and mix well together. Remove from heat and stir in sour cream. Add nutmeg, season with salt and pepper and serve immediately.

BRAISED LEEKS

These leeks go especially well with Pan Roasted Mackerel, *page 90, or with any fish* dishes.

1/2 lb. butter
4 large leeks, trimmed of all green, washed and cut lengthwise, then in 1/2-inch slices
1 medium white onion, sliced
1 bunch parsley, chopped
salt and ground white pepper to taste

Melt butter in a large pot and add leeks and onions. Cook gently, stirring, for 10 minutes until soft and juicy. Stir in parsley, add salt and pepper to taste and serve.

COLESLAW

Serve Coleslaw *with* Fish and Chips in Lager Batter, *page 84, or as a side dish on its own. This version is crunchy, tasty, and very simple to make.*

$1/4$ head each red and white cabbage, shredded, washed and drained
1 medium carrot, peeled and grated
1 medium white onion, finely chopped
$1/2$ cup mayonnaise
$1/4$ cup sour cream
2 tbs. apple cider vinegar
$3/4$ tsp. sugar
salt and ground black pepper to taste

In a large bowl, mix together cabbages, carrots and onion. In a separate bowl, combine mayonnaise, sour cream, vinegar and sugar. Add wet ingredients to vegetables and mix very well. Taste and season with salt and pepper. Refrigerate until needed.

ROASTED GARLIC PUREE

A great flavor enhancer for many dishes including soups, sauces and Mashed Potatoes, *page 61. Can be made ahead and stored in the refrigerator until needed. Try it with* Cream of Potato Soup, *page 38.*

4 large bulbs garlic
½ cup olive oil
salt and ground white pepper to taste

Heat oven to 375°. With a sharp, serrated knife, carefully cut about half an inch off the tops of garlic bulbs and lay them in a roasting pan. Drizzle oil over garlic and season lightly with salt and pepper. Cover tightly with aluminum foil and bake for about 1 hour. Remove from oven and allow to cool completely. When cool, take each bulb and squeeze out all of the cloves into a food processor, discarding remaining skin. Puree until smooth, taste and season again with salt and pepper. Transfer to a clean container and refrigerate until needed.

SAVORY SAUCES, RELISHES AND DRESSINGS

TARTAR SAUCE

Tartar sauce makes a great complement to many fish dishes, especially cod, halibut, or other white fish. Recommended with traditional Fish and Chips in Lager Batter, *page 84.*

1 cup mayonnaise
4 ounces pickled gherkins, cucumbers, onions or zucchini, finely chopped
2 hard boiled eggs, peeled and chopped
1 ounce capers
2 tbs. chopped parsley
1 tbs. chopped tarragon
1 splash Tabasco Sauce
salt and ground black pepper to taste

Combine all ingredients in a mixing bowl. Refrigerate until needed.

WHISKEY GRAVY

Serve this distinctive gravy with Roast Chicken With Champ, *page 92, or with any meat dish to give it a 'pub food' style.*

1/4 cup. butter
1/4 cup flour
2 cups *Chicken Stock,* page 3, hot
1/4 cup Irish whiskey
1/2 cup white wine
salt and ground black pepper to taste

Melt butter in a thick-bottomed pot and stir in flour. Cook gently, stirring, for 5 minutes until lightly browned. Add hot stock, whisking constantly. Bring to a boil, skim, lower heat and simmer for 10 minutes.

While gravy is simmering, in a separate pot, carefully bring whiskey to a boil and simmer for 2 minutes until alcohol has burned off. Add wine and bring back to a boil. Lower heat and simmer until reduced by 3/4. Pour into gravy pot. Stir well, taste, season with salt and pepper and remove from heat. Pass through a fine strainer and keep warm.

SAFFRON BUTTER SAUCE

This is a great sauce to pair with Almond-Black Pepper Crusted Salmon, *page 87. Saffron has a delicate and aromatic flavor.*

1 cup white wine
10 black peppercorns
4 shallots, peeled and thinly sliced
2 cloves garlic, thinly sliced
1 large pinch saffron threads
1/4 cup heavy cream
1/2 lb. butter, cut into small cubes, room temperature
salt and ground white pepper to taste
1 lemon wedge

Pour wine into a small pot and add in peppercorns, shallots, garlic and saffron. Bring to a boil, lower heat and simmer until almost dry. Add cream and simmer again for 3 minutes. Remove from heat and add butter piece by piece, whisking until completely incorporated. Taste, season with salt and pepper, squeeze in the lemon wedge and pass through a fine strainer. Keep warm.

CHILI-LIME SAUCE

This spicy-fresh sauce goes well with any fish dish, but especially with Fried Calamari, *page 26.*

1 egg yolk
1 clove garlic, finely chopped
juice of 2 limes
1/4 tsp. Colman's English mustard powder
1/2 cup olive oil
2 tbs. chili powder
salt to taste

In a food processor, combine egg yolk, garlic, lime juice and mustard powder. With the motor running, gradually pour in oil in a thin stream until mixture is the consistency of mayonnaise. Add in chili powder and season to taste with salt. Refrigerate until needed.

BÉCHAMEL SAUCE

Béchamel Sauce is one of the most traditional French sauces: it was invented by the cook of King Louis XIV. It can be made thicker or thinner, by varying the proportions of flour, butter, and milk. Serve it with the Corned Beef, Cabbage and Potato Wrap, *page 100.*

$\frac{1}{2}$ cup butter
$\frac{1}{2}$ cup all-purpose flour
1 white onion, halved, studded with cloves
2 pints milk

Melt butter in a thick-bottomed pot, add flour and cook gently, stirring, for 10 minutes. Do not brown. This is called a "roux". Remove from heat and cool slightly. Bring milk to a boil in a separate pot. Add onion to flavor milk. Return pot with roux to heat, remove onion from milk and slowly add milk to roux, stirring vigorously, until combined. Bring to a boil, stirring constantly. Lower heat and simmer gently for 8 minutes, stirring frequently. Remove from heat, taste and season with salt and pepper. Pass through a fine strainer. Keep warm if needed immediately, or cool completely and store in refrigerator.

RED WINE SAUCE

Serve this with Peppered Steaks and Country Potatoes, *page 106, or with any hearty meat dish.*

2 cups red wine
2 cups *Beef Stock*, page 4
12 black peppercorns
1 white onion, in $^1/_4$-inch dice
1 medium carrot, peeled, in $^1/_4$-inch dice
1 stick celery, in $^1/_4$-inch dice
2 cloves garlic, finely chopped
2 tbs. butter
salt and ground black pepper to taste

In a small pot, bring red wine to a boil with onion, carrot, celery, peppercorns and garlic. Lower heat and simmer until reduced by $^1/_2$. Add stock. Return to a boil and skim. Lower heat again and simmer until reduced by $^3/_4$. Remove from heat and stir in butter. Taste, season with salt and pepper and pass through a fine strainer. Keep warm.

RHUBARB RELISH

This relish works well with pork dishes, but is also worth trying with any dish where a sweet/sour flavor is appropriate, especially poultry dishes.

4 sticks rhubarb, green part removed and discarded, red part in ½-inch dice
¼ cup olive oil
1 small red onion, in ¼-inch dice
2 sticks celery, in ¼-inch dice
½ cup apple cider vinegar
1½ cups sugar
1 pinch cinnamon
salt and ground black pepper to taste

Heat oil in a thick-bottomed pot, add onion and celery and cook gently, stirring for about 5 minutes, until soft. Add vinegar, increase heat and simmer until reduced by ½, then add rhubarb. Cook, stirring, for 7 minutes, until rhubarb is soft but still retains its shape. Stir in sugar and cinnamon. Cook, stirring, for 1 more minute. Remove from heat, taste, season with salt and pepper and transfer to a serving bowl.

AIOLI GARLIC MAYONNAISE

Aioli, from Provence, is a great, garlicky accompaniment for lots of fish and meat dishes.

1 egg yolk
1 clove garlic, finely chopped
juice of 1 lemon
1/4 tsp. English mustard powder

1/2 cup olive oil
salt to taste
1 pinch cayenne pepper

In a food processor, combine egg yolk, garlic, lemon juice and mustard powder. With the motor running, gradually pour in oil in a thin stream, until mixture is the consistency of mayonnaise. Season to taste with salt and cayenne pepper.

MUSTARD VINAIGRETTE

This simple dressing, based on the Aioli Garlic Mayonnaise *recipe, above, and pairs well with* Corned Beef, Cabbage and Potato Wrap, *page 100.*

2 tsp. Dijon mustard
1/2 tsp. turmeric

1/2 cup *Aioli Garlic Mayonnaise*, page 122
2 tbs. apple cider vinegar

Combine all ingredients in a bowl and refrigerate until needed.

BACON VINAIGRETTE

This dressing is perfect with Spinach Salad with Cornmeal Fried Egg, *page 46.*

4 strips bacon, finely chopped, cooked until crispy, drained, fat reserved warm
2 shallots, peeled and finely chopped
1 tbs. Dijon mustard

¼ cup sherry vinegar
¼ cup olive oil
salt and ground black pepper to taste

In a large bowl whisk together cooked bacon, shallots, mustard and vinegar. While continuing to whisk, drizzle in reserved bacon fat and then olive oil until incorporated. Taste and season with salt and ground black pepper. Keep warm until needed.

BALSAMIC VINAIGRETTE

¼ cup balsamic vinegar
1 tsp. Colman's English mustard powder
2 shallots, peeled and finely diced

½ cup extra virgin olive oil
salt and ground black pepper to taste

In a large bowl, whisk together vinegar, mustard powder, shallots and a little salt and pepper. While continuing to whisk, slowly drizzle in olive oil and continue until all of the oil has been incorporated. Taste and season again with salt and pepper. Refrigerate until needed.

ORANGE VINAIGRETTE

This dressing goes especially well with Roasted Baby Beets, *page 55 — but try it to add tang to any leafy salad you prepare.*

½ cup fresh orange juice
¼ cup white wine vinegar
1 tsp. Colman's English Mustard powder
2 shallots, peeled and finely diced
salt and ground black pepper to taste
½ cup extra virgin olive oil

In a small pot, bring orange juice to a boil over high heat and simmer until reduced by half. In a large bowl, whisk together reduced orange juice, vinegar, mustard powder, shallots and a little salt and pepper. While continuing to whisk, slowly drizzle in olive oil and continue until all of the oil has been incorporated. Taste and season again with salt and pepper. Refrigerate until needed.

DESSERTS

Many a good meal is made memorable by the enjoyment of a fabulous dessert. These desserts all have some distinctive Irish qualities and are easy to prepare.

SODA BREAD AND BUTTER PUDDING WITH WHISKEY CUSTARD SAUCE

Servings: 4

An interesting variation on a classic, with soda bread providing that Irish flavor. Serve with Whiskey Custard Sauce.

$\frac{1}{2}$ cup unsalted butter, melted
2 large eggs, lightly beaten
2$\frac{1}{4}$ cups whole milk
1 tsp. pure vanilla extract
2 tsp. finely chopped lemon zest
$\frac{1}{2}$ tsp. cinnamon
$\frac{1}{2}$ cup granulated sugar
$\frac{1}{4}$ tsp. salt
2 cups soda bread, in 1-inch cubes
1 cup plain white bread, in 1-inch cubes
$\frac{1}{2}$ cup raisins

Heat oven to 350°. Brush four 8 oz. ramekins with melted butter as needed and set aside. In a large bowl, whisk together eggs, milk, vanilla, lemon zest, cinnamon, sugar and salt.

In a separate bowl, mix together bread, the remaining butter and raisins and add to egg mixture. Divide between the four ramekins and place in a deep, flat-bottomed baking dish. Carefully fill the baking dish half way with cold water. Bake for 1 hour, until golden brown.

WHISKEY CUSTARD SAUCE
3 egg yolks
¼ cup granulated sugar
½ cup milk
¼ cup heavy cream
2 tbs. Irish whiskey
½ tsp. vanilla extract

In a bowl, whisk together egg yolks and sugar until thick and pale yellow colored. Bring milk and cream to a boil in a saucepan and pour ½ into egg mixture, whisking gently. Mix well, then pour that mixture back into the remaining hot milk. Heat very gently, stirring constantly, until mixture has thickened.

Remove from heat, stir in whiskey and vanilla and pass through a fine strainer. Chill completely over a bowl of ice and refrigerate until needed.

DARK CHOCOLATE SOUFFLE

Servings: 4

This soufflé recipe is virtually indestructible. Once prepared, it will keep overnight in the fridge and can simply be popped in the oven 20 minutes before you want to serve it — success every time! Serve with Bailey's Irish Cream Sauce.

2 tbs. brown sugar, packed
2 eggs, separated, plus 2 more egg whites
1/4 cup heavy cream
2 tbs. granulated sugar
5 oz. bittersweet chocolate, melted
2 tbs. whiskey
Powdered sugar for decoration

Heat oven to 425° and place rack on bottom shelf. In a bowl set on a pot of hot water, whisk brown sugar, 2 egg yolks and 1 of the egg whites until thickened and hot to the touch. Transfer to an electric mixer and whip on full speed until tripled in volume. Fold in melted chocolate.

In another bowl, whip cream to soft peaks. Fold into chocolate mixture. Fold in whiskey.

In a third bowl, beat remaining 3 egg whites with granulated sugar until stiff and glossy. Fold into chocolate mixture.

Fill four 6-ounce soufflé cups with mixture and place on the bottom shelf of the oven for 20 minutes. Serve immediately with *Bailey's Irish Cream Sauce* on the side.

BAILEY'S IRISH CREAM SAUCE   Makes 1 cup

3 egg yolks
1/4 cup sugar
1/2 cup milk
1/4 cup heavy cream
1/2 tsp. vanilla extract
2 tbs. Bailey's Irish Cream

In a bowl, whisk together egg yolks and sugar until thick and pale yellow colored. Bring milk and cream to a boil in a saucepan. Pour 1/2 of milk-cream mixture into the egg mixture, whisking gently. Mix well, then pour combined mixture into remaining hot milk. Heat very gently, stirring constantly, until mixture has thickened. Remove from heat, stir in Bailey's and vanilla and pass through a fine strainer. Chill completely over a bowl of ice and refrigerate until needed.

MINT CHOCOLATE CHIP
ICE CREAM PROFITEROLES

Servings: 4

Fill these with any flavor ice cream and keep in the freezer for an impromptu treat.

1 cup all-purpose flour
¼ cup butter
1 egg
½ cup cold water
2 cups mint chocolate chip ice cream
powdered sugar for decoration
1 cup *Chocolate Sauce*

Heat oven to 425° and line a baking sheet with parchment paper.

Sift flour into a bowl and set aside. Bring water and butter to a boil. When butter is melted add flour in one go and beat thoroughly with a spatula until mixture forms a ball. Remove from the heat and allow to cool. When cool, beat in egg until completely combined.

Transfer mixture to a pastry bag with a large plain tip. Pipe onto baking sheet in 2-inch balls, making 12 in all. Press peaks down with your finger to prevent burning and place in center of oven. After 10 minutes, reduce heat to 400° and continue to cook for 20 minutes.

Remove from oven, transfer to a rack and allow to cool. When cold, cut profiteroles in half and place a scoop of ice cream inside each one. Replace top half and return to freezer to firm up ice cream. To serve, heat oven to 400°, remove from freezer and place in oven just until outsides are warm. Remove from oven, dust with powdered sugar and serve on a pool of *Chocolate Sauce.*

CHOCOLATE SAUCE

1 cup heavy cream
12 oz. semisweet chocolate, broken into small pieces

Heat cream gently in a pot until just below boiling. Remove from heat and add chocolate. Let stand for 10 minutes until chocolate has melted. Stir until smooth. Transfer to serving dish and keep warm.

BANANA CREAM PIE

There's little Irish about this dessert really — except that we like it — but it is always good to have something tropical in your repertoire. Serve this with Mango Sauce to add some tangy flavor.

2 cups whole milk
8 egg yolks
1½ cups sugar
½ cup all-purpose flour
1 cup butter, in small pieces
½ tsp. cinnamon
1 tsp. vanilla extract
3 cups heavy cream
4 bananas, thinly sliced, tossed with
    juice of 1 lemon
1 pre-baked 9-inch pie shell

In a heavy saucepan, bring milk to a boil. Using an electric mixer, beat egg yolks, slowly adding sugar, for 2 minutes, until mixture is thick and pale yellow colored. Beat in flour. Reduce speed to slow and gradually add hot milk. Mix well.

Transfer to a heavy saucepan. Bring to a boil over gentle heat, beating constantly, until mixture is very thick. Remove from heat and beat in butter piece by piece, until incorporated. Beat in cinnamon and vanilla extract. Allow to cool.

Beat cream until firm. Fold ½ of cream into egg mixture. Fold in sliced bananas and pour mixture into pie shell. Top with remaining whipped cream and chill for 2 hours in the refrigerator before serving. Serve with a drizzle of *Mango Sauce*.

MANGO SAUCE
1 ripe mango, peeled and cored
juice of 1 lemon
juice of 1 orange
1 tsp. sugar

Puree all ingredients together in a blender until very smooth. Refrigerate until needed.

IRISH APPLE TART

There's a subtlety to Irish apple tart that's hard to describe. Perhaps it's the restrained use of sugar that allows the tartness of the apples to shine through, or maybe it's the pungency of the whole cloves. Whatever it is, it's one of those decidedly Irish flavors that you'll surely find in a good Irish pub.

1$\frac{1}{2}$ lb. *Sweet Shortcrust Pastry,* recipe follows
6 Granny Smith apples, peeled, cored, sliced and tossed with the juice of 1 lemon
$\frac{1}{4}$ cup plus 1 tbs. granulated sugar
6 whole cloves
$\frac{1}{2}$ cup butter, melted
$\frac{1}{4}$ cup flour, plus more for dusting
1 egg and 2 tbs. milk, beaten together for glazing

Heat oven to 350°. Brush an 8-inch round tart pan with butter and dust with a little flour. Roll out $\frac{1}{2}$ of the pastry on a floured board and line the pan. Crimp the edges and pierce the bottom a few times with a fork. Bake for 10 minutes. Remove from oven and cool. Increase oven temperature to 375°.

Meanwhile, in a large skillet, gently cook apples in remaining butter until soft. Stir in sugar. Remove from skillet and cool completely. Fill tart crust with apples and sprinkle on cloves.

Roll out remaining pastry on a floured board and cover top of tart. Pinch the edges together, brush with egg , place in the center of oven and bake for 30 minutes. Remove from oven and allow to cool.

SWEET SHORTCRUST PASTRY

1 cup all purpose flour, sifted
$\frac{1}{2}$ cup butter, cut into small chunks
$\frac{1}{4}$ cup granulated sugar
$\frac{1}{4}$ cup ice water

In a bowl, blend butter, sugar and flour by rubbing between your thumb and fingers until mixture has the consistency of breadcrumbs. Add in water and work into a ball. Refrigerate for 30 minutes before using.

IRISH COFFEE BAKED ALASKA

Servings: 4

All the elements of an Irish whiskey-coffee, coffee and cream are de-constructed and re-assembled here in this interesting, make-ahead dish, that can keep for a week in the freezer.

¾ lb. basic sponge cake, cut into 4 equal
   rounds
2 tbs. Irish whiskey
4 large scoops espresso gelato or good
   quality coffee ice cream

3 egg whites
½ cup granulated sugar
½ tsp. vanilla extract
powdered sugar for decoration

Heat the oven to 500°. Brush sponge cake rounds with whiskey and place a scoop of gelato on each. Place in the freezer.

With an electric mixer, whip egg whites until they start to thicken. Slowly add in sugar and continue beating until mixture forms stiff peaks. Whisk in vanilla, remove from mixer and place meringue in a pastry bag with a large star tip.

Remove sponge rounds from freezer and pipe meringue around each one to form a nice swirl, completely sealing the gelato inside. Return to the freezer until needed.

To finish, remove from freezer, place on a baking sheet and bake for 10 minutes until well browned. Remove from oven, dust with powdered sugar and serve immediately.

INDEX

Serve Creative, Easy, Nutritious Meals with **nitty gritty®** Cookbooks

100 Dynamite Desserts
9 x 13 Pan Cookbook
Asian Cooking
Barbecue Cookbook
Beer and Good Food
Blender Drinks
New Bread Machine Book
Bread Machine VI
Burger Bible
Cappuccino/Espresso
Casseroles
Chile Peppers
Convection Oven
Cook-Ahead Cookbook

Deep Fryer
Dessert Fondues
Edible Gifts
Edible Pockets
Fondue and Hot Dips
Fondue, New International
Freezer, 'Fridge, Pantry
Grains, Cooking with
Healthy Cooking on Run
Ice Cream Maker
Irish Pub Cooking
Italian, Quick and Easy
Juicer Book II
Kids, Cooking with Your

Kids, Healthy Snacks for
Loaf Pan, Recipes for
Low-Carb
Pasta Machine Cookbook
Pasta, Quick and Easy
Porcelain, Cooking in
Salmon Cookbook
Sensational Skillet
Simple Substitutions
Toaster Oven Cookbook
Wedding Catering book
Wraps and Roll-Ups

"Millions of books sold—for more than 35 years" **For a free catalog, call:** **Bristol Publishing Enterprises**
(800) 346-4889
www.bristolpublishing.com